The Encyclopedia of
North American Indians

Volume I
Abenaki – Baskets

General Editor
D. L. Birchfield

Marshall Cavendish
New York • London • Toronto

Published in 1997 by
Marshall Cavendish Corporation
99 White Plains Road
Tarrytown, NY 10591-9001
U.S.A.

© 1997 by Marshall Cavendish Corporation

Developed, designed, and produced by Water Buffalo Books, Milwaukee

Project director: Mark J. Sachner
General editor: D. L. Birchfield
Art director: Sabine Beaupré
Photo researcher: Diane Laska
Project editor: Valerie J. Weber

Editors: Elizabeth Kaplan, MaryLee Knowlton, Judith Plumb, Carolyn Kott Washburne

Consulting editors: Donna Beckstrom, Jack D. Forbes, Annette Reed Crum, John Bierhorst

Picture credits: © B. & C. Alexander: 41, 42, 46; © Archive Photos: 45, 47, 52, 66, 74, 110, 114, 119, 124 (top), 130, 131, 136;
© Kit Breen: Cover, 17, 51, 75, 102, 128, 132; © Brown Brothers, Sterling, PA: 84; © 1994 Steven H. Bruno, First Image West:
135; © J. Pat Carter/Gamma Liaison: 111; © Corbis-Bettmann: 44, 67, 69, 95, 101; © Robert Frerck, Odyssey Productions: 29, 115,
117, 123; © Dirck Halstead/Gamma Liaison: 25; © Richard Hunt: 116; © 1994 Millie Knapp: 59; © 1995 Millie Knapp: 139;
© 1996 Millie Knapp: 39, 63; © David Loch/Gamma Liaison: 22, 24, 87, 88; © Buddy Mays/Travel Stock: 21; © Allen
McInnis/Gamma Liaison: title; © Moundville Archaeological Park, University of Alabama Museums: 40; © Michael
Okoniewski/Gamma Liaison: 37; © Reuters/Corbis-Bettmann: 106, 127; © REUTERS, Eric Miller, Archive Photos: 82;
© Mike Roemer/Gamma Liaison: 26, 78; © Renato Rotolo/Gamma Liaison: 80, 81; © Susan Silberberg: 20; © Elliott Smith: 35;
© STOCK MONTAGE, INC.: 58; © Stephen Trimble: 33, 65, 76, 85, 90, 91, 97, 103, 104, 105, 107, 122, 124 (bottom), 125, 143,
144; © UPI/Corbis-Bettmann: 53, 57, 64, 73, 138, 140 (both); © Michelle Vignes/Gamma Liaison: 79; © Andrew Wallace/Gamma
Liaison: 23; © 1993 S. Kay Young: 30, 61; © 1995 S. Kay Young: 93

Library of Congress Cataloging-in-Publication Data

The encyclopedia of North American Indians.
     p. cm.
    Includes bibliographical references and index.
    Summary: A comprehensive reference work on the culture and history of Native Americans.
    ISBN 0-7614-0228-4 (vol. 1)   ISBN 0-7614-0227-6 (lib. bdg.: set)
    1. Indians of North America--Encyclopedias, Juvenile.
    [1. Indians of North America--Encyclopedias.]
    E76.2.E53   1997
    970.004'97'003--dc20   96-7700
                                                 CIP
                                                 AC

Printed and bound in Italy

Title page illustration: The flag of the activist Mohawk Warrior Society flies atop a tipi erected at the site of a Native
protest in Quebec, Canada. Heavy industry, outside business interests, and widespread pollution caused by these interests have combined to disrupt the traditional lives and economies of Mohawk communities throughout Ontario, Quebec, and New York State. As a reaction to the loss of revenue and stability within their reserves and reservations, some
tribal leaders have turned to less traditional ways of making money, such as operating gaming casinos and resorts. This
in turn has fueled the conflict between Native people who prefer a more traditional way of life and those who would
push for greater assimilation into the dominant culture. In the 1990s, scenes like the one shown in this photo, in which
tribal factions, supporters from throughout North America, and government authorities square off against one another,
have become frequent in Mohawk Country, particularly on the Canadian side of the border.

Editor's note: Many systems of dating have been used by different cultures throughout history.
The Encyclopedia of North American Indians uses B.C.E. (Before Common Era) and C.E. (Common Era)
instead of B.C. (Before Christ) and A.D. (Anno Domini, "In the Year of the Lord") out of respect
for the diversity of the world's peoples.

CONTRIBUTORS

General Editor

D. L. Birchfield
Cornell University

Editorial Consultants

Donna Beckstrom
Milwaukee Area Technical College

Jack Forbes
University of California–Davis

John Bierhorst
*Author and translator in the field of
Native American Studies*

Annette Reed Crum
University of California–Davis

Authors

Susan Arkeketa
*Faculty, Haskell Indian Nations
University*

Jeannette Armstrong
Director, The En'owkin Centre

Barbara Behm
Author and Editor

John Berry
*Faculty, Oklahoma State
University*

Liza Black
University of Washington

D. L. Birchfield
Faculty, Cornell University

Kathryn Broyles
*Faculty, Concordia
International University,
Estonia*

James Bruchac
*Director, North American
Native Authors
Distribution Project*

E. K. Caldwell
Author and Journalist

Carter Blue Clark
*Executive Vice President,
Oklahoma City University*

Tom Colonnese
*Faculty, Assistant Vice President for
Minority Affairs, University of
Washington*

Shelley Davis
Editor, United Keetoowah Band
Cherokee Newspaper

Marlena Dolan
Faculty, The En'owkin Centre

Alison Farmer
University of Wisconsin–Milwaukee

Jack Forbes
*Director, Native American Studies,
University of California–Davis*

Lee Francis
*National Director, Wordcraft
Circle of Native American
Mentor and Apprentice
Writers*

Jaimie Fraser
Independent Author

Jennifer Geigel
Author

Paula Giese
Author and Editor

Roxy Gordon
Author and Journalist

Candy Hamilton
Journalist

Terri Hansen
Pacific Northwest Bureau Chief,
News from Indian
Country

Tom Heidlebaugh
Author and Journalist

Lee Hester
Faculty, Oklahoma City University

Bruce Johansen
*Faculty, University of
Nebraska–Omaha*

Patricia Lantier-Sampon
Author and Editor

Paul Larson
Faculty, Moravian College

Tom Marshall
*American Indian Studies Librarian,
University of Arizona*

Tiffany Midge
Author and Journalist

Paulette Molin
Administrator, Hampton Institute

Joel Monture
Author and Journalist

Dave Pego
Editor, Great Promise Magazine

Cornel Pewewardy
Faculty, University of Kansas

David Press
Author

Petra Press
Author and Researcher

Philip Red-Eagle
*Features Editor and Copublisher,
The Raven Chronicles*

Jim Rementer
Author

Pamela Rentz
*Contributing Editor,
Moccasin Telegraph*

Loriene Roy
Faculty, University of Texas

Mark J. Sachner
Author and Editor

W. Austin Sebastian
Author

John Smelcer
Publisher, Salmon Run Press

Mary Stout
*Director, Library Technical Services,
Pima Community College*

Jackie Winter Stringham
Author and Educator

Stephen Stringham
Author and Educator

Joel Thomason
University of Iowa

Carolyn Kott Washburne
*Faculty, University of
Wisconsin–Milwaukee*

Valerie Weber
Author and Editor

Kai Wedel
Author

Heidemarie Z. Weidner
Coordinator of Composition, Tennessee Technological University

Ron Welburn
*Faculty, University of
Massachusetts–Amherst*

Gerry William
Faculty, The En'owkin Centre

Tora Williamsen
Faculty, Oklahoma State University

Michael Wilson
*Faculty, University of
Wisconsin–Milwaukee*

Norma Wilson
Faculty, University of South Dakota

Craig Womack
*Faculty, University of
Nebraska–Omaha*

Kay Wood
*Faculty, Oklahoma State
University*

Editor's Note

As you will quickly learn from reading this encyclopedia, the cultures, civilizations, and inhabitants of Native North America have been an endless source of study and speculation among scholars, writers, and artists for centuries. From the early writings of the Spanish friar Bartholomé de Las Casas, to the relatively recent attention paid by archaeologists and anthropologists to ancient Indian artifacts and sites, non-Native scholars have long shown an abundance of interest in the indigenous peoples of the Americas. Likewise, non-Native artists have come back again and again to Native cultures, customs, and life ways as subjects of their work. From the graphic drawings that accompanied Las Casas's horrific accounts of Spain's brutalization of Caribbean Natives in the late 1400s, to the sympathetic but highly nostalgic nineteenth-century portrayals of Indians in Frederic Remington's paintings and sculptures, to the outrageous and witless Hollywood caricatures of Indians in the middle decades of the twentieth century, Native American cultures have been subjected to ceaseless interpretation and reinvention at the hands of non-Native observers.

In the last decade or so of the twentieth century, the reporting of history has taken a turn away from simplification and toward diversity. This turn toward a multicultural, multiethnic perspective has rescued from obscurity the many racial, ethnic, religious, and cultural groups, including women, that have had a profound but often neglected impact on historical and current events. Multiculturalism has become an accepted standard for academic programs from preschool through high school. Within this framework, students have begun peering at North American history and culture through a wider and more inclusive lens. In addition to bringing to light experiences and events that have traditionally taken a back seat to the dominant, Eurocentric view of culture, multicultural insights into North American history reveal our collective nature to be more rounded, more varied, and far more interesting than many of us could have imagined.

The multicultural lens has taken in a wider view of Native North America as well, with ancient Native civilizations generally recognized as ancient American civilizations. Today there is a greater appreciation of the art, images, and stories that have survived the devastating impact of European invasion, conquest, and abuse, as well as the insensitivity of the dominant European-American culture toward previous generations of American Indian peoples. Today, more than ever, indigenous peoples are acknowledged as rightful forebears to the legacies and traditions that make up the American continents.

In spite of this recent recognition, however, Native peoples continue to struggle more than any other North American ethnic groups against the view that their cultures are extinct. In the eyes of many non-Indians, the tragedy of Native North America lies in the passing of a romantic or noble Indian past at the hands of the white settlers and armies who pushed Indians westward and onto reservations or reserves until there were few Indians left and still fewer Native communities. Instead of understanding and addressing the circumstances of Indian people today, the glorification of a supposedly "vanishing" Indian past has led to what many Native observers call an "out of sight, out of mind" response to Native Americans. Despite the good intentions of the writer or reader, so long as Native cultures and people are portrayed as no longer existing, the dominant culture has no need to recognize them, understand them, address them, or fear them—hence, in the eyes of many scholars, the ease with which "dead-Indian books" have made their way to the mainstream of readers who crave information about Native North America.

The work that you hold in your hands, the Marshall Cavendish *Encyclopedia of North American Indians,* offers middle-school through young-adult readers an alternative to literature that represents Native America as a thing of the past, lumps together the hundreds of Native cultures and communities into a single ethnic group, or portrays romantic images of Indians "contributing" to European America by offering turkey and corn to early settlers. By way of contrast, *The Encyclopedia of North American Indians* explores the multitude of ways in which Native people participate in a culturally diverse North America even as they continue to uphold their various traditions and maintain their identity as members of specific nations and tribes.

Organized in a traditional encyclopedia format (ten volumes of alphabetically ordered entries and an eleventh volume containing appendices and indexes), this set features entries on a range of subjects of historical and contemporary significance. The entries range in length from a few paragraphs to several pages. The longest entries—

those of two or three thousand words—cover subjects of broader significance, such as children, Native culture areas of the Americas, the role of families in Native societies, federally recognized nations and tribes, unrecognized nations and tribes, European attitudes toward indigenous peoples, European colonialism, Indian activism and resistance, Native American foods and cooking, Native governments, U.S. Indian policy, Indian concepts of labor, Native American contributions, the so-called Indian wars, government-Indian treaties, and ceremonial regalia.

Other longer entries cover subjects related to the arts, entertainment, and popular culture. Longer entries on broadly defined groups of contemporary Native writers from certain tribes or geographical regions are intended to steer readers in the direction of more literature by and about North American Indians. In addition to the larger entries on contemporary writers, the encyclopedia is filled with many shorter entries on specific Native authors, many of them at the peak of their careers. Entries of varying length also cover other areas of cultural expression, such as theater, beadwork, architecture, philosophy, jewelry, games, toys, broadcasting and journalism, silversmithing, quillwork, dancing, storytelling, featherwork, music, singing, drumming, and festivals and powwows. Throughout the encyclopedia, images of Indian art, both traditional and contemporary, dramatize Native cultural expression as not just a thing of the past but as a living component of Indian Country today.

Longer entries on European attitudes and colonialism are complemented by specific entries dealing with racial attitudes and perceptions, with such subjects as "firewater," Hollywood imagery, scalping, and the so-called tomahawk chop. Shorter entries on specific personalities, as well as on conflicts, social conditions, health-related issues such as alcoholism and other illnesses, Indian activist movements, government policies, treaties, legislation, and court cases affecting Indian people, all provide specific treatments of subjects dealt with in broader strokes in the longer entries. A special effort has been made to relate these and other subjects both to their historical antecedents and to their role in contemporary Native life.

In addition to entries on every U.S. state and Canadian province and territory, the encyclopedia also contains specific entries on indigenous peoples and cultures throughout the Americas, including Mexico, Greenland, the Caribbean, Central America, and parts of South America. In all cases, through both the discussions and the illustrations, readers gain an understanding of the historical past and the present reality of life in Indian Country.

Readers are guided to finding discussions of related topics in a variety of ways. Most entries contain references to other articles in the encyclopedia, and many of the medium-length and longer entries feature suggestions for further reading. As readers follow the succession of "See also" references from entry to entry, they will discover a fascinating web of relationships among the many topics concerned with historical and contemporary Indian life. In volume eleven, the final volume, readers will find, in addition to a general index to the encyclopedia as a whole, special indexes guiding them to material in a variety of areas, including U.S. states, Canadian provinces and territories, and other countries throughout the Americas; specific nations and tribes; individual personalities from a variety of fields and walks of life; historic and archaeological sites; and legislation, treaties, and court decisions involving Indian America.

In addition to the indexes, volume eleven also includes a selective bibliography of further readings on several subjects and a number of appendices. The appendices include lists covering the following subjects: federally recognized U.S. Native nations and tribes; recognized Native entities within the state of Alaska; U.S. Indian reservations; reservation, tribal, and council business office names, addresses, and phone numbers; unrecognized U.S. nations and tribes; Canadian Native bands; contemporary U.S. and Canadian Native periodicals, television and radio stations, publishers, and news sources; Native centers, museums, and landmarks in the United States, Canada, Puerto Rico, and Mexico; and a calendar of Native events in the United States and Canada. Other appendices include a map of and guide to the historical and anthropological culture areas of the Americas; a guide to the pronunciation of tribal names; and a ranking of states, provinces, and territories according to their Native populations. Of special interest is a discussion and map of Nunavut, a new Inuit territory to be carved out of the eastern half of Canada's Northwest Territories.

In addition to the editorial, design, photo research, and production staff members who worked long and hard in bringing *The Encyclopedia of North American Indians* into being, a sizable number of scholars, educators, authors, and editorial consultants contributed their talents to the conceptual groundwork, writing, editing, and reviewing of the pages that follow. Most of these contributors are members of Native communities throughout the United States and Canada, and they bring a broad range of professional and personal experience to bear on their areas of interest and expertise.

Of the nearly sixty authors and consultants commissioned to contribute to this encyclopedia, nearly forty— almost two-thirds—are Indian writers from a variety of creative and professional backgrounds. They include university professors and administrators, artists and craftspeople, historians, editors, journalists, storytellers, musicians, librarians, directors of museums and other Native cultural centers, and public educators. They come from an even wider range of Native backgrounds, including such tribal and community origins as Abenaki, Ahtna Athabascan, California Karuk, Cherokee, Chickasaw, Choctaw, Comanche/Kiowa, Conoy/Cherokee, Creek, Hunkpapa Sioux, Powhatan/Lenape (Delaware), Mohawk, Nebraska Winnebago, Ojibwe (Chippewa), Okanagan, Oneida, Otoe-Missouria, Potawatomi/Peoria, Pueblo, Saginaw Chippewa, Santee Sioux, Shawnee, Sisseton-Wahpeton/Klallam, Spallumcheen, United Keetoowah Band Cherokee, and White Earth Chippewa. As a group, they have contributed more than 80 percent of the text that appears in these pages.

Thanks in large part to the cultural diversity of the authorship, readers of this encyclopedia will undoubtedly be struck by the diverse viewpoints that emerge from the entries themselves. The writers and editors have made a conscious effort to engage their subjects from an "Indian" vantage point. To put it simply, a wide range of historical events, personalities, and geographical entities are discussed in the encyclopedia. And all of them— from Indian boarding schools to African-Americans and other non-Indian ethnic groups, to such European-American figures as Andrew Jackson, Abraham Lincoln, Buffalo Bill, and Barbara Crabb—are examined from the viewpoint of the Native peoples and cultures whose lives they intersect. These entries, along with entries on Indian activism, literature, social conditions, and other subjects of current interest, direct the reader to a view of life in North America as it comes down to the experience of being a Native North American.

Despite the current interest in Native cultures among non-Natives, the gains made by North American Indians in the past few decades have been hard fought and, by the measure of many, somewhat meager. Most of these gains have been won in legal battles to regain sovereignty over land and resources once guaranteed Indian people in treaties long since ignored or broken by federal, state, and provincial governments. Despite these victories, North American Indians have had to fight against an array of laws, norms, and attitudes that often render them isolated—some would say invisible—within the dominant North American culture. By virtue of its focus on subjects of both historical and contemporary interest, its diverse collection of editors and writers, and its forthright attitude concerning the condition of being a Native American, *The Encyclopedia of North American Indians* takes issue with the invisibility and isolation fostered by the mainstream. This work draws a multifaceted portrait of North American history and society, and it does so in words and pictures that give a living voice to the indigenous peoples who have long formed the cultural underpinnings of the American continent.

D. L. Birchfield, General Editor

A Note about the General Editor

The encyclopedia's general editor, D. L. Birchfield, a member of the Choctaw Nation of Oklahoma, is a writer and editor who holds a Juris Doctor degree and is presently teaching in the American Indian Program at Cornell University. He is a widely published writer of fiction, humor, and various forms of nonfiction who has served on the editorial staffs of many Native American periodicals. He is executive secretary of the National Advisory Caucus for Wordcraft Circle of Native American Mentor and Apprentice Writers and has helped conduct workshops for Native writers on college and university campuses throughout the continent.

Contents

VOLUME 10

ABENAKI

For at least ten thousand years, the people known as the Abenaki, meaning "People of the Dawn," have lived in what are now the northeastern United States and southeastern Canada. Before the coming of the Europeans, the Eastern Abenakis—a large tribal group that includes the Penobscots, Androscoggins, and Wawencocks—lived in present-day Maine. The Western Abenakis—another tribal group that includes the Missisquois, Pennacooks, Winnipesaukees, Sokokis, and Cowasucks—lived in present-day Vermont and New Hampshire, known to them as Ndakinna, meaning "Our Land." These groups all were, in turn, a part of the Wabanaki, a confederacy of nations that originally called themselves Woban-ki, from which the name Abenaki, or "People of the Dawn," is derived. The Wabanaki, all with similar languages and cultures, include not only the Eastern and Western Abenakis but also such neighboring tribes as the Passamaquoddy and the Maliseet of present-day eastern Maine and New Brunswick, and the Micmac of present-day Nova Scotia.

The Abenaki language is from the Algonquian language family. Traditional Abenaki houses include the wigwam, which was the more temporary structure, and the longhouse, which was used in larger, more permanent settlements. The Abenakis raised a variety of food crops suited to the cool northern climate; they also hunted and fished, never killing more game than they needed to survive. To take the best advantage of their varied food supply, the Abenakis moved from place to place in a seasonal pattern. However, they regularly returned to centralized longhouse villages for winter festivals and other social events, and to gather their forces during times of war. The Abenakis often traveled by means of birch-bark canoe on the many lakes and rivers of their lands.

A traditional dancer of the Penobscot tribe of Indian Island, Maine. The Penobscots are currently the only federally recognized Abenaki group in the United States.

The Abenakis were one of the first Native nations to encounter Europeans in North America, and they soon found themselves fighting for their very survival. By the 1760s, the Abenakis had fought five wars against the English in an effort to stop the massive invasion of their lands. Because of the competition and tension created by the fur trade, the Abenakis also had to constantly defend themselves against the often better-armed nations of the Iroquois. In an effort to protect themselves and their lands, the Abenakis often sided with the French in their long struggle against the English for control of North America. The Abenakis earned a reputation as fierce warriors, especially during the Seven Years' War (1756–1763). This war between England and France, which was called the French and Indian War by the English colonists, ended in defeat for the French and their Indian allies. During and after periods of warfare, many Abenakis moved farther and farther north, either to escape the conflict or because they had been defeated. Because of these migrations, Abenaki reserves such as Saint Francis (Odanak) were set up by the French in Quebec, Canada. The reserves exist to this day.

By 1763, Abenaki populations throughout North America had been decimated by years of war and disease. Following the Revolutionary War (1775–1783), the Abenakis who chose to stay on their traditional lands received no mercy from non-Native settlers, who ignored Abenaki rights to the land. Today, the only federally recognized Abenaki community in the United States is the reservation of the Penobscots of Indian Island in Maine. However, various unrecognized Abenaki groups still exist in Vermont, New Hampshire, Massachusetts, and New York. One of the largest and most visible communities is that of the Missisquoi Abenakis in Swanton, Vermont.

— J. Bruchac

SEE ALSO:
Algonquian; Bruchac, Joseph; Federal Recognition; French and Indian War; Iroquois Confederacy; Longhouse; Maine; Massachusetts; Micmac; New Brunswick; New Hampshire; Nova Scotia; Passamaquoddy; Penobscot; Unrecognized Nations and Tribes; Vermont; Wabanaki Confederacy; Wigwam.

SUGGESTED READINGS:
Bruchac, Joseph. *The Faithful Hunter: Abenaki Stories*. Greenfield Center, NY: Greenfield Review Press, 1988.
Calloway, Colin G. *The Abenaki*. New York: Chelsea House, 1989.
——— . *The Western Abenakis of Vermont, 1600–1800 War, Migration, and Survival of an Indian People*. Norman: University of Oklahoma, 1990.
Speck, Frank G., and Wendell Hadlock. *Penobscot Man: The Life History of a Forest Tribe in Maine*. Philadelphia: University of Pennsylvania Press, 1940.

ABROGATION OF TREATIES

See Treaties, Indian–United States.

ACCULTURATION

Acculturation is the process of adopting the customs of another culture, either through education or force or a combination of both. When a Native American culture such as the Kwakiutl or Lakota is forced to give up its ceremonies and language and accommodate the demands of a larger society, acculturation is the intended goal of the intrusive greater society.

When the Europeans arrived on the Atlantic Coast and met many different Native cultures, they applied social and economic pressure to these First Nations, or Native Americans, in an effort to make them adapt to the Europeans' needs. The social pressures included forcing various tribes to choose sides in European conflicts carried across the ocean to North America. Throughout the seventeenth and eighteenth centuries, Native people became embroiled in conflicts such as the French and Indian War (the name given by English colonists to the conflict that pitted England against France and its Native allies) and intertribal struggles such as those between the Huron (Wyandot) and the Iroquois Confederacy. Other social pressures on First Nations included having to adapt to Europeans settling in large numbers on their lands. Native Americans also had to maintain their sense of community in the face of rapid change forced on them by the European invasion.

The economic pressures suffered by Indians were slightly more subtle. As the Europeans advanced, they brought coffee and sugar, guns and gunpowder. They traded with Natives for animal pelts and food produce, altering traditional Native systems of exchange until the First Nations developed a dependency on European goods. Because the Narragansetts or the Shawnees did not have an economy based on the relationship between supply and demand and other factors with which Europeans were familiar, they were forced to adapt dramatically in order to compete with other tribes for access to European weapons and metal goods.

The 1800s were characterized by huge, usually catastrophic, upheavals in traditional Native cultures. This was the era of treaties between various Native groups and the governments of the United States and Canada, and, particularly in the United States, of the breaking and ignoring of these treaties by the government, soldiers, and settlers. This was also the era of removal, the U.S. policy of uprooting eastern tribes from their homelands and moving them west, principally to the Indian Territory, an area that includes present-day Oklahoma. In the 1800s, the U.S. government also pursued the policy of allotment, in which tribal lands were broken up and distributed to individual members of the tribe for personal ownership and then opened up to non-Native settlement. One huge effect of allotment, in addition to the diminishing of tribal land bases, was the breaking up of tribal identity.

With the arrival and continued presence of the Europeans from the colonial era into the nineteenth century, East Coast nations adapted and changed. Similar changes were taking place among the coastal tribes of the Pacific Northwest and in the Southwest for the Pueblo, Apache, and Navajo peoples. A great deal of the trade with the Europeans was in animal pelts, and thus the beaver and eventually the buffalo, both crucial to trade, almost became extinct.

After almost five hundred years of determined efforts to take away land, a sense of a cohesive community, and a variety of cultural characteristics from the Natives of North America, new methods of acculturation were employed after the times of war and treaty-breaking were past. These included the infamous boarding schools, which separated children from their families for years at a time, and the failed policies of the War Department and the Bureau of Indian Affairs, such as termination. The boarding schools served as a massive effort to destroy the old languages, the deep community bonds, and the cultural ties that taught children how to be part of the ancient traditions. Termination more directly served to separate Indian peoples from their land base, forcing them to sell at extremely low prices or give away their ancient lands and rights.

By the mid-twentieth century, the image of Indians as "Vanishing Americans" and other notions of Native America as a place that existed only in the past tense implied that the acculturation efforts of the United States and Canadian governments were suc-

ceeding. Since that time, however, there has been a great wave of resurgence of culture among Native people from the Abenakis of New England to the Tongva of the Los Angeles Basin. Where boarding schools attempted to make Native peoples forget their past, the elders continued to tell stories. Where termination was enacted on the Klamath or the Menominee Nations, concerted efforts brought the tribes back to life. Acculturation—either as a subtle pressure or a formal government policy—has failed as each tribe in North America continues to regain its cultural values and rights.

— T. Heidlebaugh / P. Red-Eagle

SEE ALSO:
Abenaki; Apache; Boarding Schools; Bureau of Indian Affairs; French and Indian War; General Allotment Act; Iroquois Confederacy; Klamath; Menominee; Narragansett; Navajo; Pueblo; Removal Act, Indian; Shawnee; Termination Policy; Trail of Tears; "Vanishing Americans"; Washington Coast and Puget Sound Indians, History of; Wyandot.

ACOMA PUEBLO

The Acoma are a Keresan-speaking Pueblo people. The other Keresan-speaking Pueblos are the Cochiti, Laguna, San Felipe, Santa Ana, Santa Domingo, and Zia Pueblos. Acoma Pueblo, now commonly known as Old Acoma, is also called the "Sky City." It sits atop a 400-foot-high (121-meter-high) mesa approximately fifty miles (eighty kilometers) west of Albuquerque, New Mexico. It was built about 1000 B.C.E. Along with some of the Hopi villages farther west in Arizona, Acoma Pueblo is probably the oldest continuously inhabited settlement within the present boundaries of the United States.

At the time the Spanish arrived in the Southwest in the sixteenth century, there were between seventy and one hundred pueblos in what is now the state of New Mexico. Acoma is one of the nineteen pueblos that still remained at the end of the Spanish colonial era. It is one of only five (along with Pícuris, Taos, Zuni, and the ancient villages of the Hopi) that had not been forced to change its location. Geographically, it is a western pueblo. Only the Zunis and the Hopis are to be found far-

An outdoor stairway at Acoma Pueblo, New Mexico.

With origins dating back to about three thousand years ago, Acoma and its stone houses sit atop a mesa, leaving little doubt as to why this pueblo has also been called "Sky City."

ther west. But it is more appropriately considered an eastern pueblo because of its linguistic ties with the other Keresan-speaking Pueblo people of New Mexico. Like all of the pueblos in New Mexico (except Zuni), Acoma is located in the watershed of the upper Rio Grande.

Acoma, along with most of the other Pueblo Nations, chose not to reorganize its traditional form of government under the Indian Reorganization Act of 1934. Instead, it retains a traditional Pueblo form of tribal government. At Acoma, the Antelope Clan has the responsibility of providing tribal leaders. A cacique—a religious official—also bears many responsibilities that non-Native Americans associate with governmental functions. Acoma poet, short story writer, and editor Simon J. Ortiz, one of the most accomplished Native American literary writers, served as interpreter and first lieutenant governor of Acoma in the 1980s.

The Acoma people hold title to about 375,000 acres (151,875 hectares) of land. Recent population reports for the Acoma people have not been consistent. The 1980 U.S. Census reported an Acoma population of 3,592. The 1989 Bureau of Indian Affairs Labor Force Report counted 4,350. The 1990 census reported a population of 2,435. Only about fifty people now inhabit the ancient town of Old Acoma year-round. It has no electricity or running water. Most of the Acoma people live in the nearby communities of Acomita, Anzac, and McCarty's. A visitor center with a museum, crafts shop, and restaurant is located at the foot of the mesa. A tribal bingo hall is also located nearby.

SEE ALSO:

Cacique; Coronado Expedition; Hopi; Indian New Deal (Indian Reorganization Act); Keresan Pueblos; New Mexico; New Spain; Ortiz, Simon J.; Pueblo; Spain; Taos Pueblo; Zuni.

SUGGESTED READING:

Minge, Ward Alan. *Acoma: Pueblo in the Sky*, 2nd ed. Albuquerque: University of New Mexico Press, 1991.

ACQUIRED IMMUNE DEFICIENCY SYNDROME

See AIDS.

ACTIVISM, INDIAN

Political and civil rights activism among Native American people has existed since the Europeans first set foot in North America. Since that time, and during the centuries that followed, Native peoples have been actively involved in the struggle to survive as distinct cultural groups with political and economic rights within the larger North American population.

American Indian people have fought for their tribal and survival rights in many different ways. They have battled within a variety of governmental arenas and within state courtrooms. In the eigh-teenth and nineteenth centuries, they used their skills as military strategists on the battlefields. In the last century, they fought politically on city streets and in reservation communities, gathering advocates and sympathizers for their many important causes.

Since the earliest centuries of American history, Native people have fought to eradicate government injustices, resisted forced removal from their ancestral lands, fought to uphold their treaties, and promoted the enforcement of tribal rights and sovereignty. Through all of their battles, they have met with great resistance from most U.S. political leaders.

One of the earliest Native American rights organizations was a national women's group founded in 1879, called the Women's National Indian Association, led by Mary L. Bonney and Amelia S. Quinton. This organization was committed to the keeping of treaties, to education, and to establishing missionary and social welfare activities.

AIM leader Russell Means *(right)* and other Indian activists from throughout North America gather at Oka, Quebec, to support local Mohawk Indians in 1990. Like many Mohawk communities on both sides of the U.S.–Canadian border, the Kanesatake Mohawks of Oka have been hit hard by the heavy industry and pollution that have strained their traditional lifestyles and livelihoods.

From the late 1800s to the early 1900s, members campaigned to arouse public opinion and to influence congressional decisions on major reforms.

In 1882, Herbert S. Welsh and Henry Pancoast founded the Indian Rights Association. They advocated for education, legal protection, and land rights. They also devised plans to organize and operate as a group that would gain the respect of both the U.S. Congress and the public. They established a far-reaching correspondence network, a Washington office to monitor legislation and regulate the administration of Indian affairs, a commission of lawyers to help in drawing up legislation and operate legal cases, and an information program for the public.

Another Indian activist organization, the Lake Mohonk Conference of the Friends of the Indian, was begun in 1883 by Albert K. Smiley, a member of the Federal Board of Indian Commissioners. The series of Lake Mohonk conferences were designed to provide a forum for discussion, debate, and decision making among members consisting of humanitarian reformers, new members of the rights organization, officials in government, academics, and other influential advocates for Indian rights.

The roots of formal Indian rights movements were reflective of the social climate of the late 1800s, when several new political reforms in regard to Indians were taking place in the United States. The Dawes Act (also known as the General Allotment Act), which was passed in 1887, divided tribal land into 160-acre (64-hectare) plots and deeded them to Native families. The act was put into effect to encourage Native people to form the "habits of civilized life," to use the land for farming and raising livestock. The government believed that the Dawes Act would eventually force Native Americans to assimilate into mainstream U.S. society by con-

Tipis and placards stand before Parliament in the Canadian capital of Ottawa, Ontario, in February 1995. They were erected by Indian activists protesting living conditions on Canadian reserves and demanding tax-free status for Canadian Natives.

verting them to Christianity, securing Indian ownership of private property, providing citizenship, and providing education that would enable the Indians to become self-reliant and productive members of the dominant society.

With the exception of the National Indian Defense Association, virtually all of the earliest Native American rights organizations were in agreement with the Dawes Act. They were in favor of education, the land allotments, and many of the other reforms that the Dawes Act provided, including the eventual dissolution of tribes. But in regard

Mohawk and other Native activists in Quebec line a barricade set up by the Canadian Army to control protesting over issues of tribal leadership and the intrusion of non-Native business, industry, and political influence into Native communities.

to Indian citizenship, the different rights organizations were divided. It was not until 1924 that the Indian Citizenship Act was passed, declaring all Indians to be citizens without affecting any of their rights to tribal or other property.

But citizenship was not the same as being eligible to vote. The right to vote was decided by state laws, not Congress, so voting rights for Indians varied from state to state. Discriminatory laws within some states prevented Indian people from voting until as late as 1948.

It is important to note that all of the early Indian rights organizations were composed of European-Americans. It was not until the start of the 1900s that Native voices began to be heard within formal congressional arenas, as more and more American Indians were speaking English, acquiring education, and acculturating into, or becoming more a part of, the dominant society.

Many of these emerging "educated" Indians founded the Society of American Indians in Columbus, Ohio, in 1911. One of the founding members was Dr. Charles Eastman, a Wahpeton Sioux whose father had been sentenced to death for having been part of the Great Sioux Uprising in Minnesota during the 1860s. Charles Eastman went from a missionary school to Dartmouth College in New Hampshire and Boston Medical School, later becoming a prolific writer of well-received books concerning the plight of Native Americans. Another founder was Dr. Carlos Montezuma, a Yavapai, who was educated in Brooklyn and Urbana, Illinois. Later, he became a physician in the Indian Health Service. He was a passionate and controversial speaker, referring to reservations as "houses of destruction." There was also Arthur C. Parker, a Seneca and a descendant of the religious reformer and prophet Handsome Lake. Parker was an ethnologist, archaeologist, editor, writer, and museum official. He once said that "the true aim of educational effort should not be to make the Indian a white man, but simply a man, *normal to his environment.*"

The Society of American Indians opened a Washington, D.C., headquarters; established a periodical that eventually came to be known as the *American Indian Magazine;* organized a National Indian Day; presented an annual essay contest for Native students; and provided platforms for Native voices and opinions to be heard. The society also sought support for a bill introduced by Charles D. Carter (Chickasaw) that would organize a committee to codify Indian law and determine the exact legal status of Native American tribes and their members. The society also petitioned to open the U.S. Court of Claims to the tribes and investigate educational reform and ways to improve health facilities.

Native American women played an important role in paving the road for modern Native American rights activism. Among these strong leaders were Susette and Susan LaFlesche of the Omaha tribe. They were from a family that consisted of accomplished anthropologists, teachers, writers, doctors, artists, poets, librarians, and religious officers. Susette LaFlesche was educated in Elizabeth, New Jersey, and later became a teacher in her reservation's school. She became an effective spokesperson for the Ponca Nation when members were driven off their ancestral lands, helped influence legislation that stopped the forcible removal of Native tribes, and influenced a Supreme Court decision stating that "an Indian is a person." Susan LaFlesche, younger sister to Susette, was a physician during a time when even Euro-American female doctors were a rarity; she was highly committed to fighting for Native causes.

In the 1960s and 1970s, events like this—large-scale marches and demonstrations over Native-rights issues—were common. Such marches drew Native activists and various non-Indian supporters from throughout the United States.

In February 1993, Native activists gathered in South Dakota to remember the twentieth anniversary of the occupation of Wounded Knee in 1973. The issues that motivated activists in the 1970s—tribal leadership and self-determination—continue to be a concern for Native people today.

Laura Cornelius of the Oneida tribe was another female activist devoted to Native rights, refusing to "genuflect before the altar of white progress." A fierce opponent of large cities and their economic, technical, office, and factory systems, she proposed that communities center on industries that would blend with the environment to ensure that the wilderness would be protected. It was her feeling that the existing systems were unnatural and would fail in the end.

In addition to the Society of American Indians, other Indian rights groups were organizing in the early twentieth century, including the Alaska Native Brotherhood, founded in 1912; the Grand Council Fire of Chicago, founded in 1923; the American Indian Association, formed in 1922; the National Council of American Indians, founded in 1926; and the Indian Defense League of America in 1926, which established the right of Indians to pass freely across the U.S.–Canadian border.

The 1930s were regarded as the New Deal era, and many Indian reform organizations began negotiating for the Indian Reorganization Act (IRA), which passed Congress in 1934. This act's main thrust was to correct the failures of the Dawes Act of fifty years earlier. The new reform of the IRA was most concerned with reducing federal control of Indian affairs and restoring Native American nations' self-government and self-determination. It also advocated support of traditional Native American culture.

After World War II, the focus shifted within the Indian rights movements because of the contributions made by Native Americans during wartime. In 1944, the National Congress of American Indians (NCAI) was founded and became one of the most important Native rights movements in the country, with Indian representatives from twenty-seven states, many of whom were World War II veterans.

In the years following World War II, protests increased against the U.S. government and, in particular, the Bureau of Indian Affairs. Many public works projects threatened Native landholdings and areas that were sacred to Native people. The Iroquois Confederacy was opposed to many water and power projects that would have had a destructive effect on their land. During the 1940s and 1950s, the Senecas made protests and began legal battles against the Kinzua Dam project in Pennsylvania. In the 1950s and 1960s, the Mohawks and Tuscaroras organized resistance to the St. Lawrence Seaway project in New York.

At the beginning of the 1960s, protesters in the Pacific Northwest were fighting for their fishing rights, which were guaranteed by treaty. These protests were called "fish-ins," and they sought to end the legal restrictions on Northwest tribes' access to fishing. These protests increased public awareness through strong media coverage and attracted many supporters like comedian and political activist Dick Gregory and actor Marlon Brando. The fish-in movement eventually won a legal victory for fishing rights in the Northwest. It also became a model for American Indian activism, which increased dramatically along with other civil rights movements and protests of the 1960s.

In the 1960s, Indian activism reached an all-time high; more and more urban Indians joined organizations and protests. These activist organizations were the National Indian Youth Council (NIYC), founded in 1961, and the American Indian Movement (AIM), founded in 1968. Each of these movements instilled a renewed sense of pride in Indian people who had felt the loss of a tribal identity, particularly those who had been raised in Indian boarding schools and those who had assimilated into urban areas. This emergence of Native pride was referred to as "Red Power."

From 1975 to 1977, the decline of Red Power movements corresponded to a renaissance in federal Indian policy. During this time, the American Indian Policy Review Commission made tours and examined Indian conditions on reservations and in cities throughout the United States. Federal legislation was passed that abolished the termination policies of the 1950s and sought to confirm tribal self-determination. In 1971, the Alaska Native Claims Settlement Act (ANCSA) was an important legislative act that recognized the land rights of Alaskan Natives and made provisions for mineral royalty payments, land transfers, and land payments. Federal Indian policy regarding Native rights and tribal self-determination enabled tribes to conduct their affairs by more independent means.

Indian activism during the 1980s brought many tribal issues to the forefront through legal negotiations in courtrooms. The number of Native attorneys increased, and tribal communities became more sophisticated in dealing with complex legal problems within the court system. The legal issues facing Native American communities during this time focused upon self-determination rights, unsettled land claims, and the repatriation (return to the tribe of origin) of Indian remains and artifacts.

Indian rights movements and activism can most readily be defined as organizations concerned with defending, modifying, or changing governmental policies in regard to Native affairs. The relationship between American Indians and the United States government has come through gradual and dramatic changes and will continue to shift and grow for as long as the United States stands as a nation. With the increasing number of Native representatives in U.S. government, along with a wider public sensitivity to Native rights, the issues of change and reform should create better and fairer policies for Native American people.

— T. Midge

SEE ALSO:
Alaska Native Claims Settlement Act; American Indian Movement; American Indian Policy Review Commission; Bureau of Indian Affairs; Dawes Commission; Eastman, Charles; Fishing Rights; General Allotment Act; Indian New Deal (Indian Reorganization Act); Iroquois Confederacy; Montezuma, Carlos; Parker, Arthur; Picotte-LaFlesche, Susan; Reburial and Repatriation of Human Remains and Sacred Objects; Self-determination; Self-determination Policy; Sioux Uprising (1862); Termination Policy; Trail of Broken Treaties; Treaties, Indian–United States.

SUGGESTED READINGS:
Avery, Susan, and Linda Skinner. *Extraordinary American Indians*. Chicago: Children's Press, 1992.

Brown, Dee. *Bury My Heart at Wounded Knee.* New York: Holt, 1970.

Champagne, Duane. *Native America: Portrait of the Peoples.* Detroit: Visible Ink Press, 1994.

Dorris, Michael. *The Paper Trail: Essays.* New York: HarperCollins Publishers, 1994.

Erdoes, Richard. *Crying for a Dream.* Santa Fe, New Mexico: Bear & Company Publishing, 1989.

Hertzberg, Hazel W. "Indian Rights Movement, 1887–1973." *Handbook of North American Indians:* Vol. 1 of *History of Indian–White Relations.* Washington, DC: Smithsonian Institute, 1988.

Jones, Jayne Clark. *The American Indian in America.* Vol 2. Minneapolis: Lerner Publications Company, 1973.

Nabokov, Peter. *Native American Testimony.* New York: Viking Penguin, 1991.

ADENA CULTURE

Adena is a name archaeologists have given to an Eastern Woodlands culture that was centered in the Ohio River Valley and reached its peak about 100 B.C.E. The Adena were the earliest Mound Builders in the East. The culture is named for an archaeological site in Ohio where most Adena sites are found—more than two hundred of them so far in southern Ohio and in neighboring portions of Indiana, Kentucky, West Virginia, and Pennsylvania.

Adena Culture began to emerge by about 700 B.C.E. By 400 C.E., it had disappeared in Ohio, but it may have survived at sites in West Virginia until as late as 700 C.E. It was succeeded by another mound-building culture called Hopewell, which, in turn, was succeeded by a temple mound culture known as Mississippian, which was still active when Europeans arrived.

Because Adena artifacts had been found at archaeological sites along the Atlantic seaboard and elsewhere, Adena Culture was once thought to extend over a much broader geographical area than is now generally accepted. It is now believed that these Adena artifacts were acquired in trade in exchange for raw materials from those areas, such as mica and shell, which the Adena used for making ceremonial and ornamental items.

Adena mounds are of a number of different types. Many are burial mounds, but many also form geometric patterns that seem to be enclosures. Some of these are large circles, squares, or pentagons, while others follow the natural curve of a hill. Many of these enclosures are up to 330 feet (100 meters) in diameter. They enclose burial mounds that sometimes have interior ditches, giving the mound the appearance of being protected by a moat. The largest Adena mound is 68 feet (21 meters) high and is located near Miamisburg, Ohio.

The Adena are thought to have built the largest effigy mound in North America, the Great Serpent Mound in southwestern Ohio. About 20 feet (6 meters) wide and from 2 to 5 feet (0.6 to 1.5 meters) high, it stretches for 1,130 feet (343 meters) along a ridge overlooking Brushy Creek. Recently, attempts have been made to impound Brushy Creek to create a recreational complex, which has resulted in organized protests so that the Great Serpent Mound may remain undisturbed in its natural environment.

The Adena also made pottery, but it was of a practical kind; they did not expend a lot of creative energy decorating or refining it, and it did not play an important role in burial rites. Instead, pipes and ornaments are often found in burial sites.

The Adena may also have invented printing—if that is the purpose for which they used the small, hand-size, engraved tablets that are commonly found in their burial sites. The tablets are usually carved with designs consisting of curves or abstract animals. Printing is the use of a mold to stamp something on another object. The minting of coins is an example of printing. It is thought that the Adena may have filled the tablets with pigment and stamped the designs on their bodies or on cloth, which would constitute printing. Many ancient cultures have invented printing, usually in the form of the minting of coins, without realizing its vast potential for other kinds of communication. Even ancient cultures possessing highly literate members, such as the Greek scholars who toiled in the great library at Alexandria in Hellenic Egypt, arduously copying manuscripts by hand, had the knowledge of printing, in the form of minting coins, without realizing its potential for the mass reproduction of manuscripts.

The Adena participated in an extensive network of trade and were especially skilled at working copper imported from the north. They fashioned intricate copper luxury items, including beads, bracelets, rings, gorgets (ornamental collars), and axes. At one site, a twenty-eight pound (thirteen-kilogram) ceremonial copper ax was found.

Many Adena sites were ruined in the nineteenth century by amateur archaeologists who looted them for their artifacts. Unknown numbers of others have been destroyed by U.S. land-use practices, including highway construction, urban sprawl, mechanized agriculture, and inundation by reservoirs. Early non-Indian homesteaders in the region showed little interest in the mounds, and very little was done to either protect them or study them systematically before many of them had been destroyed.

It is not known whether the Hopewell Culture, which succeeded the Adena Culture, was the result of the migration of new people into the region, or whether the Hopewell people were the descendants of the Adena. The two existed side by side for a time, so a case can be made either that Adena Culture gradually evolved into Hopewell Culture, with the changes taking place at different rates in different places, or that the Hopewellians were a different people who gradually supplanted the Adena.

— D. L. Birchfield

SEE ALSO:
Hopewell Culture; Mississippian Culture; Mound Builders; Serpent Mound.

AFRICAN-AMERICANS

The term *African-American* and its closely related predecessor *Afro-American* have both been used to refer to people of African or part-African ancestry living in the Americas and especially in the United States. Generally, the term *African-American* is used to describe people descended from the brown-skinned peoples of Africa, those who also call themselves Black or Black Americans, and not for those descended from the lighter-colored peoples, of some parts of North Africa, such as Algeria or Morocco, which are considered Arab nations. The term never seems to be used for people born in Africa with European ancestry, such as white people from South Africa,

A collection of ancient Olmec funerary figures, from Mexico's Natural Museum of Anthropology. Artifacts such as these, with human figures bearing ethnic features that have been described as African, have led some scholars to speculate about the possibility of early African explorations of the Americas.

Like many Americans, Joe Smith, shown in a portrait dressed in regalia as a grass dancer in 1993, is of mixed ethnic descent. A member of the Blackfeet Nation, he is also able to claim African ancestry.

tral America, or South America, are of mixed racial ancestry. Only some of these people's ancestors were from Africa; many also have Native American ancestors. Some have European ancestors, and a smaller number also have Asian ancestors. An unknown proportion of African-Americans are of unmixed African ancestry; however, this is hard to determine except for people whose immediate parents were both born in Africa. This is because many African-Americans who have Native American ancestry mixed with their African ancestry can look quite African since one inherits characteristics from any or all of one's four grandparents.

Many experts believe that Africans first reached the Americas in very ancient times, using ocean currents that could easily bring watercraft from the Canary Islands and Cape Verde Islands off Africa to South America and the southern Caribbean Sea. This belief has, as one might expect, been a source of some controversy among various scholars, especially as it affects the usual theories about early Norse explorers who are now considered to have preceded Columbus by several hundred years in voyaging to the Americas from Europe. The colossal Olmec heads found in Vera Cruz, Mexico, sculpted in around 1000 B.C.E., are often described as being Africanlike, although they might also resemble some Pacific Island peoples and certain Native American cultures.

Later evidence, such as murals and ceramic heads in Mexico, seem to depict people who have African features or black color. In 1492 to 1493, Christopher Columbus learned of black-colored people who were trading in guanin (a gold-copper alloy) in the Caribbean. In 1513, the Spaniard Vasco Núñez de Balboa is said to

Kenya, Namibia, or other countries on the African continent.

In the past, words such as *negro, preto* (both meaning "black"), and *colored* have been used in North America to refer to African-Americans, while words such as *mulatto, zambo, moreno, morisco, pardo, griffe, grifo,* and many other similar terms have been used to refer to people of mixed African and Native or European descent in various parts of North and South America.

Many African-Americans, whether living in the United States, Canada, the Caribbean, Cen-

have seen African people living in the interior of Panama near the Native American city of Cuarecua. Thus, it is very possible that Africans long preceded Europeans in the Americas, but very few mainstream scholars have come to accept the evidence.

In any case, it is certain that Africans were among the first non-Native Americans to settle in the area of the United States. In the 1520s, Africans were taken to Chicora (South Carolina) by the Spaniards, where they rebelled and remained when the Spaniards left. One African man married a Native American "queen," and he and his wife were still living in 1539 to 1541 when Hernando de Soto brought still other Africans to the southern United States, along with Mexican and Caribbean Natives. In 1565, persons of African descent were among the first settlers of St. Augustine, Florida, while other Africans or part-Africans were left behind or escaped from Spanish expeditions in the Southwest and present-day Kansas.

In the early 1500s, the Spaniards brought many people of African descent to Haiti, Cuba, Mexico, Peru, and other regions. Some were Muslims from northern Africa, as was the famous Esteban (Estevanico), who traveled across North America with Cabeza de Vaca in the 1520s. Many Africans were free or were of mixed race, but others were brought in as captives (slaves). Those captives often rebelled and joined with Native groups to fight against the Spaniards as in Mexico, Haiti, Ecuador, Colombia, Venezuela, and Brazil, where the famous *quilombo* (free republic) of Palmares existed for many decades, with both Africans and Tupí (indigenous) people living there.

During a four- or five-hundred-year period, a great deal of intermarriage took place between Native Americans and Africans. Many Native Americans were captured by the English, French, Spanish, Dutch, and Portuguese and were sold into slavery. As slaves, they were thrust together with Africans and people of mixed ancestry, and eventually children called mulattos were born. The mulattos were almost always of mixed Native American and African racial ancestry in the early colonial period. Such mulattos were also known as *zambos*, *lobos*, *pardos*, *cafusos*, and many other names, depending on the region and the individual's color. If European ancestry was present, other terms were also used.

Many Africans and mixed-ancestry people also ran away to Native nations or to Native American towns. Sometimes Native nations also had African slaves, especially the Cherokees, Chickasaws, Creeks, and Choctaws. These same tribes also had indigenous captives as well, but they seem to have usually sold these captives to non-Indian slave traders in return for arms and European goods. In any case, a great deal of intermixture took place between Native Americans and Africans, especially along the Atlantic Coast from Florida to Massachusetts, in Oklahoma, and in countries such as Mexico, Panama, Venezuela, Guyana, Colombia, Peru, Chile, Argentina, and Brazil. Significant African-Native American mixture also has occurred in Puerto Rico (Borinquen), Cuba, and Haiti, and throughout Central America and the Caribbean.

Today, there are several hundred million people in the Americas who are of mixed African and Native American descent, many also having some European or Asian ancestry. The people called "African-Americans" are only a small part of this group, the other people being identified as Latin Americans, such as Mexicans, Brazilians, Cubans, or Puerto Ricans, or as members of Native American groups.

— J. D. Forbes

SEE ALSO:

America and *Americans*; American Indians; Columbus, Christopher; De Soto Expedition; Five Civilized Tribes; Olmec.

SUGGESTED READINGS:

Forbes, Jack D. *Africans and Native Americans: The Language of Race and the Evolution of Red-Black People.* Champaign/Urbana: University of Illinois Press, 1993.

Johnston, James Hugo. *Race Relations in Virginia and Miscegenation in the South.* Amherst: University of Massachusetts Press, 1970.

Katz, William L. *Black Indians: A Hidden Heritage.* New York: Atheneum, 1986.

Littlefield, Daniel F. *Africans and Creeks.* Westport, CT: Greenwood Press, 1979.

———. *Africans and Seminoles.* Westport, CT: Greenwood Press, 1977.

———. *The Cherokee Freedmen*. Westport, CT: Greenwood Press, 1978.
———. *The Chickasaw Freedman*. Westport, CT: Greenwood Press, 1980.

AGRICULTURE, NATIVE AMERICAN

While popular imagination sometimes stereotypes Native Americans as nomadic hunters, many, if not most, of North America's Native peoples practiced agriculture, the domestication of plants for human consumption. At least half of Earth's staple vegetable foods, the most important being corn and potatoes, were first cultivated by American Indians, who often drew their sustenance from hunting, gathering, *and* agriculture. By 800 C.E., agriculture was an established way of life for many Native peoples in North America.

Native American agriculture has influenced eating habits around the world so completely that many people forget their culinary origins. Before the voyages of Christopher Columbus, the Italian food of today with its tomato-based sauces was unknown. The Irish cooked their food without potatoes. Europeans satisfied their sweet tooths without chocolate. Corn was unknown outside the Americas, as were peanuts. These crops were produced by many Native American cultures' experiments over thousands of years. Knowledge of plant life was passed along from generation to generation with other social knowledge, usually by the elder women of a Native tribe.

The production of food was also woven into American Indian spiritual life. Often corn and beans—which grow well together because the beans, a legume, fix nitrogen in their roots—were said to maintain a spiritual union. Among the Iroquois and many other Native peoples, for example, festivals celebrated the role of the "three sisters" (corn, squash, and beans). Archaeologists tell us that the food complex of corn, beans, and squash was transferred northward from Mexico as a set of rituals before it was an agricultural system. By practicing the rituals, Native Americans in the corn-growing areas of North America became farmers.

Corn was first domesticated in the highlands of Mexico about seven thousand years ago from a wild grass called *teosinte*. The first corncobs were the size of a human thumbnail. As the use of maize ("Indian corn") spread north and south from Mexico, Native peoples domesticated hundreds of varieties and bred them selectively so that the edible kernels grew in size and numbers. Corn requires a 160-day frost-free growing season; the northern limit of corn cultivation also often marks the limit of intensive Native agriculture.

Corn, the major food source for several agricultural peoples across the continent, enjoyed a special spiritual significance. Some peoples, such as the Omahas of the eastern Great Plains, "sang up" their corn through special rituals. In addition to "singing up the corn," the Pueblos cleaned their storage bins before the harvest, "so the corn will be happy when we bring it in." The Pawnees grew ten varieties of corn, including one, called "holy" or "wonderful" corn, that was used only for religious purposes and never eaten. The Mandans had a Corn Priest who officiated at rites during the growing season. Each stage of the corn's growth was associated with particular songs and rituals, and spiritual attention was said to be as important to the corn as proper water, sun, and fertilizer. Among the Zunis, a newborn child was given an ear of corn at birth and endowed with a "corn name." An ear of maize was put in the place of death as the "heart of the deceased" and later used as seed corn to begin the cycle of life anew. To Navajos, corn was as sacred as human life.

Corn is intertwined with the origin stories of many Native American peoples. The Pueblos say that corn was brought to them by Blue Corn Woman and White Corn Maiden, who emerged to the surface of the earth from a great underground kiva, a sacred place. At birth, each infant is given the seed from an ear of corn as a fetish to carry for life as a reminder that the Corn Mothers brought life to the Pueblos. The corn fetish has a practical side as well: Should a harvest completely fail for drought or other reasons, the fetishes may become the seed corn for the next crop.

Many Native peoples offer prayers of consent, sufferance, or forgiveness of the plants as well as the animals that they consume, out of a belief that the essence of life that animates human beings also

An Arizona Hopi man works a cornfield of the Eagle Clan. For many American Indian peoples, the cultivation of land has long been viewed as a way of establishing a common bond among various members of a tribe or clan.

is present in the entire web of animate and inanimate life and objects. Long before a science of "sustained yield" forestry evolved, Native peoples along the Northwest Coast harvested trees in ways that would assure their continued growth as part of a belief that the trees are conscious beings. Some Native Americans charted farming cycles through complicated relationships with the sun and moon and through rites and other celebrations. In addition to domesticating dozens of food plants, they also harvested the wild bounty of the forests for hundreds of herbs and other plants used to restore and maintain health.

While the Mayas are known for their temples in such places as Tikal, Copan, and Palenque, most Mayas—the commoners who supported the small elite that maintained the temples—spent a large part of their time cultivating food, principally corn. Most of the Mayan ceremonial centers were surrounded by very large earthworks for agriculture.

These artificial ramparts were not discovered by modern archaeologists until they started exploring satellite images of the land, since today the earthworks are very difficult to see from ground level. The earthworks included complex irrigation channels and raised fields, often hewn from reclaimed swampland. The Mayas dredged nutrient-rich soil from the bottoms of the irrigation ditches to fertilize fields that they raised above the flood level of the rainy season. The fields were so rich that they produced several crops a year to feed the urban areas.

The discovery of complex agricultural earthworks among the Mayas caused scholars to question earlier assumptions that the Mayas had practiced slash-and-burn agriculture, which was said to have deforested the land, exhausted and eroded the topsoil, and played a role in the collapse of the "classic" age of the Mayas. Today, the collapse of the Maya culture is seen as caused not by the destruction of the forest by farming, but by damage to the environment and an increase in social disorganization caused by increasing warfare between city-states. Not all of the Mayas' earthworks were constructed to aid agriculture; some ramparts were defensive. As war became more common and deadly, the Mayas' complex agricultural system suffered immensely.

About the same time that the Mayan civilization collapsed, the ancestors of today's Pueblos were building a corn-based culture in the Chaco Canyon of present-day New Mexico. The Pueblos of the Rio Grande are the cultural and economic inheritors of the Mogollon, Anasazi, and Hohokam communities to the west and southwest of the upper Rio Grande Valley. Cultivation of corn was introduced into the area about 3000 B.C.E., and about 2000 B.C.E., beans and squash were added. Cotton later became a third staple crop.

Also about two thousand years ago, irrigation was introduced to supplement dry farming in the area, and irrigation of farmland is the key factor in Pueblo land use. The Pueblos took advantage of brief heavy precipitation by constructing some of their irrigation works to collect rain runoff at the bases of the steep cliffs. In order to plan, construct, and maintain elaborate land systems, cooperation between several villages was crucial. Irrigation systems need routine maintenance, so nonkinship associations were created to cope with such work. This organizational framework had other community functions, and it revolved primarily around the spiritual life of the Pueblos. The basic rationale for the nonkinship associations was irrigation, however. The residents of this area also constructed roads that often ran for hundreds of miles (kilometers) to provide a way to share food surpluses— if one pueblo had a bad harvest, others would make it up.

The cultivation of corn in Chaco Canyon supported a civilization that constructed the largest multifamily dwellings in North America. Such a high degree of agricultural organization also supported a culture that dominated the turquoise trade in the area. Turquoise was important as a liquid asset, a medium of trade. Pueblo centers such as Pueblo Bonito became centers of trade, manufacturing, and ceremony.

Following the Spanish colonization of New Mexico, access to water became a crucial cause for conflict. Land without water was worthless in the arid Southwest. Paradoxically, the Pueblos in 1680 used the waters of the Rio Grande to defeat the Spanish; they staged their revolt while the river was flooding to keep Spanish reinforcements out.

Some Native peoples used fire to raze fields for farming and to drive game while hunting. These were not fires left to blaze out of control, however; Navajos who used range fires customarily detailed half of their hunting party to contain and control the fire and to keep it on the surface, where the flames would clear old brush so that new plant life could generate, instead of destroying the forest canopy. Donald Hughes, in *American Indian Ecology*, points out that when Europeans first laid eyes on North America, it was much more densely forested than today: "Eastern America was a land of vigorous forests, not a fire-scarred wasteland." The parklike appearance of many eastern forests was a result of Native peoples' efforts to manage plant and animal life, not a totally natural occurrence.

Although a majority of Native peoples did not possess a concept of individual landownership, their rituals and rites, as well as their daily lives, displayed a reverence for the land with which their agriculture was so closely intertwined. Land was typically (but not always) held in common by a particular group—clan, tribe, or Native nation. In the Cherokee language, the word that means "land" (*eloheh*) also denotes culture, history, and religion.

At first sight, many immigrating Europeans did not recognize Native American agriculture because it did not resemble their own. Indians did not domesticate draft animals and only rarely plowed their fields. Sometimes crops were grown in small clearings amid forest.

When colonists arrived in eastern North America, many of the Native peoples they met farmed corn in large tracts. John Winthrop, governor of the Massachusetts Bay Colony, admired abandoned Native cornfields and declared that God had provided the epidemic that killed the people who had tended them as an act of divine providence, clearing the way for the Puritans. Surviving Native Americans taught the Puritans which seeds would grow in their territory. Most of the seeds that the

Puritans had brought from England did not sprout when planted in the area that the colonists called "New England."

In the Southeast, in coastal Georgia, the Yamassees cultivated gardens near lagoons and marshes where hills of corn, beans, and squash were grown several feet (meters) apart. Soil exhaustion demanded that these cultivated areas be rotated periodically. Moving villages to adjacent bluffs and islands in the same locale every five to ten years seemed to have been a standard pattern. Most Yamassees lived in small groups of a few families numbering 80 to 120 people. Several of these groups lived along a river, sound, or lagoon. Because of this subsistence structure, women's activities focused on gathering roots and nuts in the fall and winter.

Many ethnic groups that immigrated to the Americas came from agricultural or other kinds of rural backgrounds, and many, like the Italians, Irish, Poles, and Jews of Europe—as well as the Mexicans who came to work the farms and ranches of the Southwest—became urban dwellers after several generations of living in America. Likewise, many African-Americans have a long history of life in an agricultural setting, some as the descendants of rural slaves or indentured servants, some as the descendants of freedmen who ran their own farms. And yet, today, while many Black Americans live in rural areas and carry on the farming traditions of their ancestors, many more have long since moved out of "the country" and into the large and small cities of industrial North America. Like other cultures throughout North America, today's Native American societies are a mix of many kinds of livelihoods, not all of them by any means agricultural. And where Native people do farm for a living, they, like other Americans, do so by combining the traditional ways, attitudes, and methods of their culture with the necessary advances of modern equipment and science.

— B. E. Johansen

SEE ALSO:

Anasazi; Chaco Canyon; Columbian Exchange; Hohokam; Kiva; Mandan; Maya; Mogollon Culture; Native American Contributions; Navajo; Omaha; Pawnee; Pueblo; Pueblo Revolt of 1680; Zuni.

An elder from Zuni Pueblo, New Mexico, shakes pollen from a cornstalk. Corn has long been a staple of Pueblo life in the Southwest, both for its practical uses and for its spiritual significance.

SUGGESTED READINGS:

Thomas, David H. et al. *The Native Americans: An Illustrated History.* Atlanta: Turner Publishing, 1993.

Brandon, William. *American Heritage Book of Indians.* New York: Dell, 1961.

Deloria, Vine, Jr. *God Is Red.* Golden, CO: North American Press, 1992.

Dozier, Edward P. *The Pueblo Indians of North America.* New York: Holt, Rinehart & Winston, 1970.

Grinde, Donald A., Jr., and Bruce E. Johansen. *Ecocide of Native America.* Santa Fe: Clear Light, 1995.

Hughes, J. Donald. *American Indian Ecology.* El Paso: Texas Western Press, 1983.

Sando, Joe S. *The Pueblo Indians.* San Francisco: Indian Historian Press, 1976.

Underhill, Ruth. *Red Man's Religion: Beliefs and Practices of the Indians North of Mexico.* Chicago: University of Chicago Press, 1965.

AIDS (Acquired Immune Deficiency Syndrome)

The first cases of Acquired Immune Deficiency Syndrome (AIDS) among Native Americans, including Alaskan Natives, were reported before 1984. By the end of 1993, there were over eight hundred reported cases among this population.

Infectious disease epidemics have played an important role in Native American history since 1492. Europeans landing in North America brought diseases that decimated Native American nations, among them measles and smallpox.

But AIDS is one of the most serious infectious diseases ever to affect humans all over the world. It destroys the immune system, which is the main system the body uses to fight disease. At the present, there is no known cure for AIDS, and no vaccine to protect people from infection. Although various types of drug therapy, including combinations of certain drugs, have shown some signs of fighting HIV (Human Immunodeficient Virus), the virus that causes AIDS, at the present most, if not all, of those infected with HIV will die of the disease.

The majority of those infected are young, between the ages of twenty and forty. Native American teenagers and elders have also been infected, either from injecting drugs with needles carrying the virus, or from having sex with someone carrying the virus. In the past, many people also became infected with the AIDS virus by having transfusions of blood carrying HIV, but contemporary blood-screening techniques have virtually eliminated blood transfusions as a way of contracting AIDS.

American Indians and Alaska Natives are at special risk of infection by the AIDS virus because of high rates of alcohol and drug abuse (which promote poor decision making about sexual matters) and high rates of other sexually transmitted diseases (STDs), such as syphillis, gonorrhea, and chlamydia. The best protection against AIDS is not using drugs (especially with needles), and either not having sex at all, or having sex with one person only—a person who has only had sex with you. The more people one has sex with, the more danger there is of being exposed to AIDS or other sexually transmitted diseases. For those having sex, it is extremely important to use latex condoms. They are over 90 percent effective in protecting people from the AIDS virus.

Fortunately, the AIDS virus is not spread casually. For example, you cannot get it through the air, from toilet seats, from being bitten by mosquitoes that have also bitten people infected with AIDS, or by sharing drinking glasses with an infected person. It is important for people to learn, both as a matter of safety and as a matter of treating people with HIV fairly, that the only way of getting the disease is through sex or sharing needles (which may pass another person's infected blood into your body). Also, a mother with HIV can give it to her child at birth.

For Native Americans, as for other groups in which economic factors often have an effect on their health and well-being, stopping AIDS means improving Native American health. It means changing behavior that is the root of most major Native American health problems, like alcohol and other drug abuse. In addition to affecting the ability to make clear decisions about having sex, alcohol and drugs also keep the immune system from working properly. Changing one's behavior by making healthy decisions can stop AIDS and fetal alcohol syndrome (FAS), reduce teen pregnancies, and improve the quality of life for Native people and Native American communities. Making healthy decisions also means taking personal responsibility for one's own health.

AIDS is now a fact of life for all of us. This disease will undoubtedly be with us for the rest of our lives and for that of future generations. Even with advances in medically treating people with AIDS or HIV, the only way to save lives is to prevent people from becoming infected in the first place.

SEE ALSO:

Alcoholism; Children; Epidemic Diseases; Fetal Alcohol Syndrome; Indian Health Service; Smallpox.

AIM

See American Indian Movement.

AKWESASNE NOTES

The newspaper *Akwesasne Notes* was founded in the late 1960s as part of the present-day reassertion of American Indian activism. Since then, the bimonthly *Akwesasne Notes* has been one of the foremost Native-owned editorial voices for American Indian rights in the United States and Canada. In a trade where advertising pays most of the bills, this newspaper carries nearly none. At a time when newspapers have come to resemble cousins of television, it rarely publishes color, relying instead on pages dense with text. In a media world of megacorporations, *Akwesasne Notes* operates on a shoestring budget. It rarely pays contributors or editors and fiercely maintains its editorial independence.

The name *Akwesasne Notes* comes from its location on the Akwesasne (St. Regis) Reservation, a Mohawk reservation that straddles the borders of New York and the Canadian provinces of Ontario and Quebec. In addition to reporting on events throughout Indian Country, the paper has carried stories on the reunion of Native people who took part in the occupation of Alcatraz Island in San Francisco Bay, California; reports on a heated intellectual debate over whether the Iroquois Great Law helped inspire the United States Constitution; a report from indigenous peoples in Australia contributed by a Mohawk family who visited there; the latest plans for coal mining on the Hopi Reservation; and an account of negotiations between Nicaraguan Native people and the Nicaraguan government. Other articles have reported on repression of Tibetan natives by the Chinese and the organization of chapters of the environmentally activist Green Party in the United States. *Akwesasne Notes* also has described Native resistance to the destruction of Brazil's rain forests, detailed accounts of human-rights violations in Guatemala, reported trade agreements between American Indian tribes and third-world nations, discussed a proposed world constitution, and editorially supported Greenpeace, an international group of environmental activists.

The circulation of *Akwesasne Notes* averages

A barricade erected by Mohawk residents of the Akwesasne (St. Regis) Reservation proclaims their support for greater self-determination. *Akwesasne Notes* has been in the forefront of reporting—and commenting on—issues that have caused controversy and conflict among Native people throughout North America.

about ten thousand copies per issue. Most subscribers get the paper by mail. The publication has a geographic reach that few newspapers can match, with copies being mailed to indigenous people and their supporters around the world.

The newspaper's content reflects its global approach to issues involving indigenous rights, but the focus of its coverage remains the Haudenosaunee ("People of the Longhouse"). This is the Native name for the confederation of Indian nations that the French called the Iroquois and the English called the Six Nations. The coverage is honest and reports on all aspects of life for Native peoples, not just the positive ones. The pages of *Akwesasne Notes* contain candid accounts not only of internal dissension but also of occasional murder and fraud, along with graphic descriptions of the abysmal living conditions on many reservations.

On January 9, 1988, a firebomb razed the newspaper's offices during violence related to gambling and the struggle for tribal leadership at Akwesasne. Installed in a new office with equipment donated by a worldwide network of supporters, *Akwesasne Notes* did not miss a single issue, even though it sustained two hundred thousand dollars in uninsured losses from the fire.

The fire gutted the Nation House that had been the newspaper's home for much of the previous two decades. In spring 1988, in its first editorial after the fire, *Akwesasne Notes* wrote: "Our offices were torched by those amongst us here at Akwesasne who oppose our reporting on the conflicts that are plaguing the Haudenosaunee [Iroquois] nations . . . . With the gambling, the cigarette smuggling, the violence . . . it is understandable why those criminal elements amongst us are opposed to a free press disseminating information about the illegal and immoral activities around us . . . . They almost succeeded in putting us out of business . . . but we will survive." During 1991, following more gambling-related turmoil at Akwesasne, the newspaper stopped publishing. It resumed in early 1995.

SEE ALSO:
Akwesasne (St. Regis Reservation), Pollution of; Alcatraz Island, Occupation of; Constitution, United States; Iroquois Confederacy; Mohawk; Mohawk Warrior Society.

AKWESASNE (ST. REGIS RESERVATION), POLLUTION OF

Akwesasne (also called the St. Regis Reservation) is a Mohawk reservation that straddles the border of New York and the Canadian provinces of Ontario and Quebec. Within the living memory of a middle-aged person today, Akwesasne has become a toxic dumping ground riskier to human health than many urban areas. These environmental circumstances have, in two generations, descended on a people whose whole way of life had been enmeshed with the natural world. Ironically, Akwesasne is the place where the Iroquois origin story says the world took shape on a gigantic turtle's back. Today, environmental pathologists are finding turtles at Akwesasne that are so polluted, they qualify as toxic waste.

In 1985, the Mohawks requested that Ward Stone, a wildlife pathologist for the New York State Department of Environmental Conservation, conduct an environmental tour of the area. When Stone began examining animals at Akwesasne, he found that toxins such as PCBs, insecticides, and other chemicals were not being contained in the dumps that had been designated for them. After years of use, the dump sites had leaked. The toxins had gotten into the food chain of human beings and nearly every other species of animal in the area. The Mohawks' traditional economy, based on hunting, fishing, and agriculture, had been literally poisoned out of existence.

The Mohawks started Stone's environmental tour of Akwesasne with a visit to one of the General Motors waste lagoons, a place on some maps called "unnamed tributary cove." Stone gave it the name "contaminant cove" because of the amount of toxic pollution in it. One day in 1985, at contaminant cove, the environmental crisis at Akwesasne assumed a new, foreboding shape. The New York State Department of Conservation caught a female snapping turtle that contained 835 parts per million of PCBs. This was especially upsetting because the turtle carries a special significance among the Iroquois, whose creation story describes how the world took shape on a turtle's back. In fact, to this day, many Iroquois call North America "Turtle Island."

While no federal standards exist for PCBs in turtles, the federal standard for edible poultry is

Toxins collected from this plant on the Akwesasne (St. Regis) Reservation and dumped into local bodies of water designated as waste lagoons have led to numerous health, environmental, economic, and social troubles for the Mohawk reservation.

three parts per million, or about one-third of 1 percent the concentration in that snapping turtle. The federal standard for edible fish is two parts per million. In soil, on a dry-weight basis, fifty parts per million is considered hazardous waste, so that turtle contained roughly fifteen times the concentration of PCBs necessary, by federal standards, to qualify its body as toxic.

During the fall of 1987, Stone found another snapping turtle, a male, containing 3,067 parts per million of PCBs in its body fat—one thousand times the concentration allowed in domestic chicken and sixty times the minimum standard for hazardous waste. Contamination was lower in female turtles because they shed some of their own contamination by laying eggs, while the males stored more of what they ingested.

In 1985, Stone, working in close cooperation with the Mohawks, found a masked shrew that somehow had managed to survive in spite of a PCB level of 11,522 parts per million in its body. This was the highest concentration that Stone had ever

seen in a living creature, 250 times the minimum standard to qualify as hazardous waste. Using these samples and others, Stone and the Mohawks documented that Akwesasne was one of the worst PCB-pollution sites in North America.

The harmful effects of the pollution affected many aspects of life at Akwesasne. In 1986, for example, pregnant women were advised not to eat fish, historically the Mohawks' main source of protein, from the Saint Lawrence River. And until the 1950s, Akwesasne had been home to more than 100 commercial fishermen and about 120 twenty farmers. By 1990, fewer than 10 commercial fishermen and 20 farmers remained.

The U.S. Environmental Protection Agency released its Superfund cleanup plan for the General Motors foundry during March of 1990. The cleanup was estimated to cost 138 million dollars, making the General Motors dumps near Akwesasne the costliest Superfund cleanup job in the United States. It was designated number one on the EPA's "most-wanted" list as the United States' worst toxic dump. By 1991, the cost was scaled down to 78 million dollars, but the General Motors dumps were still ranked as the most expensive toxic cleanup.

"We can't try to meet the challenges with the meager resources we have," said Henry Lickers, a Seneca who is employed by the Mohawk Council at Akwesasne. Lickers also has been a leader in the fight against fluoride emissions from a nearby metal-producing plant and a mentor to younger environmentalists at Akwesasne. "The next ten years will be a cleanup time for us, even without the money," said Lickers.

Lickers also credits the destruction of Akwesasne's environment with spawning a deadly battle among Mohawks over high-stakes gambling and smuggling. After living by traditional means such as hunting and fishing became impossible, some Akwesasne Mohawks turned to earning their living by smuggling cigarettes, liquor, and weapons across the border from Canada. Profits from smug-gling financed the construction of high-stakes casinos in the area during the late 1980s. "A desperation sets in when year after year you see the decimation of the philosophical center of your society," Lickers said.

The Mohawks are not alone. Increasingly, restrictive environmental regulations enacted by states and cities are bringing polluters to Native reservations. "Indian tribes across America are grappling with some of the worst of its pollution: uranium tailings, chemical lagoons and illegal dumps. Nowhere has it been more troublesome than at . . . . Akwesasne," wrote Rupert Tomsho, a reporter for *The Wall Street Journal*.

— B. E. Johansen

SEE ALSO:

Akwesasne Notes; Iroquois Confederacy; Mohawk; Turtle Island; Uranium Mining (Navajo).

Mound State Monument, near Moundville, Alabama, preserves the art and architecture of the Mound Builder culture that once thrived in parts of North America.

ALABAMA

Alabama became a U.S. state in 1819 and is named after the Alabama Indians. *Alabama* means "I made a clearing" in the language of the Alabama people. The name came from the principal town of the tribe, which was built on the banks of the Alabama River.

There is a long history of Native Americans living in what is now Alabama. The Russell Cave National Monument at Bridgeport dates Indian inhabitation to 7000 B.C.E. There are also many Mound Builder Culture sites in Alabama; the best-known site is Mound State Monument near Moundville. The Mound Builder Culture was in decline by the early 1500s.

The first European contact in Alabama occurred in 1519, when Alonso Alvarez de Piñeda explored Mobile Bay. At the time of contact, four major Indian groups lived in Alabama: the Chickasaws in the northwest; the Cherokees in the northeast; the Creeks in the center and southeast; and the Choctaws in the southwest. After de Piñeda, the next contact with Europeans took place when Hernando de Soto ravaged the area with a Spanish army of five hundred men. On October 18, 1540, de Soto fought a Choctaw force under Chief Tuscaloosa. Spanish accounts describe a huge victory. Choctaw accounts describe the battle as more of a draw. In any case, Spanish troops moved farther west after the battle, and no permanent European settlement was established in Alabama until 1711, when the French moved into the area and began seizing land and started a town at the site of present-day Mobile.

After the American Revolution, Native people in Alabama experienced greater and greater pressure from U.S. incursion. In the early 1800s, the Creek War raged from 1813 to 1814, and Andrew Jackson and his troops defeated the forces of the Creek Confederacy at Horseshoe Bend on March 27, 1814. Horseshoe Bend National Military Park is located near Dadesville and commemorates the battle.

During the 1830s, almost the entire Native population of Alabama underwent a forced removal to Oklahoma. Only one small reservation, at Poarch Creek, has been maintained.

The 1990 U.S. Census lists 16,506 Indian people who live in Alabama, which ranks the state as twenty-fifth among states in Native American population.

SEE ALSO:
Cherokee; Chickasaw; Choctaw; Creek; De Soto Expedition; Jackson, Andrew; Mound Builders; Removal Act, Indian.

Summer in downtown Anchorage, Alaska. With only one reservation in all of Alaska, many Native people live in the cities and in communities that have retained a traditional character.

ALASKA

Alaska is the forty-ninth U.S. state. Its name is taken from the Russian version of an Aleut word, Alakshak, with several meanings—a peninsula, land that is not an island, and/or great lands. Most anthropologists believe that four major indigenous groups crossed the land bridge that once lay across the Bering Strait and made Alaska their home. They are the Aleuts; the Upiks and Inuit

Another view of the Anchorage area: ski and float planes on Hood Lake overlooked by the Alaska Range Mountains.

(Eskimos); the coastal Tlingits and Haidas; and the Athabascans. Although this theory of migration from Asia is the most widely accepted accounting for the earliest settlement of the America, others dispute the idea that the indigenous American peoples were actually "immigrants" from another part of the world. Some believe that, rather than a "bridge" of land connecting Asia and America, the land now covered by the waters of the Bering Strait was actually an enormous expanse, perhaps as wide as one thousand miles (sixteen hundred kilometers) across. It is thus possible that, rather than using the land as a migratory bridge to get from one place to another, indigenous people actually inhabited this subcontinental region, which is called Beringia, for hundreds or even thousands of years. And thus, Beringia may have been a place from which today's Native peoples moved—freely and over great expanses of time—back and forth across the present northernmost areas of Asia and America, including Alaska. In the words of some contemporary Native scholars, this would mean that "the footprints go in both directions" across Beringia, and the usual notions of the origins of Native American cultures coming from Asia to America would not necessarily be true.

The Native inhabitants of Alaska first had contact with Europeans in 1740 to 1741 when Captain Vitas Bering, a Dane employed by the Russians, reached Alaska. He brought back word to Russia of waters filled with sea mammals. Russian fur-trading vessels sailed to the Aleutian Islands and Alaskan coasts, and fur traders invaded village after village, forcing the Aleuts to supply them with furs. Many Inuits, Tlingits, and other Alaskan Native groups fought back, but it is estimated that over 90 percent of the original population was lost to murder or disease.

During the 1800s, many Alaskan Natives began to trade for European goods such as guns, knives, kettles, and cloth. They also fell victim to European diseases and to alcohol. However, some of the Inuit groups in the central part of Alaska had no contact with Europeans or Euro-Americans until the early 1900s.

The Tlingits' ongoing fight against the Russian invaders and fur traders to preserve their furs and their lands helped the Russians decide to sell Alaska to the United States for 7.2 million dollars in 1867. Secretary of State William H. Seward arranged for this huge land purchase, often known as Seward's Folly, though the land's strategic location and valuable animal and probable mineral resources made the purchase a tremendous bargain. For the next twenty years, United States governance of the area was limited.

During the 1880s and 1890s, fish canneries were established and severely disrupted Native Alaskan life. Non-Natives took over the best fishing sites and brought in their own labor. Gold prospectors discovered a huge load near Juneau in 1880, which led to an explosion of gold prospecting in the 1890s. In 1912, Alaska became a U.S. territory, the same year that the Tlingits founded the Alaska Native Brotherhood, one of the earliest of the modern-day Native organizations.

Over the next nearly fifty years, corporations took over much of the mining and mineral explorations in Alaska. During World War II, military construction was on a large scale, and afterward, the oil industry boomed.

Alaska became a state on January 3, 1959. On December 18, 1971, the Alaska Native Claims Settlement Act (ANCSA) was signed into law. Under this act, Alaska Natives received 962 million dollars and 44 million acres (17.8 million hectares) of land, but they gave up claims over the remaining 335 million acres (136 million hectares). Instead of establishing reservations, as was the practice in the lower forty-eight, thirteen regional corporations were formed to develop economic projects for their shareholders, the Native Alaskans and their descendants.

According to the 1990 U.S. Census, the Alaska Native population was 85,698, approximately 15 percent of the entire Alaskan population. This makes Alaska the fifth most populous state in terms of Native population. However, the state of Alaska contains only one Native American reservation, established by Congress in 1891—Annette Island Reserve at Metlakatla for the Tsimshian.

SEE ALSO:
Alaska Native Claims Settlement Act; Alaska Natives; Aleut; Beringia; Haida; Inuit.

ALASKA NATIVES

About eighty-six thousand Alaska Natives live in Alaska, the northernmost U.S. state. These are the people who first lived in Alaska long before Columbus happened upon the Americas in 1492. In fact, the Natives of the Americas may have been on the continent for as long as thirteen thousand years, perhaps as long ago as thirty thousand years, according to some scientists.

The Native people of Alaska fall into four distinct cultural-linguistic groups: The Inuit of the northern and southern Arctic regions; the Aleuts of the Aleutian chain of islands, which stretch far out into the Pacific Ocean; the Athabascan Indians of the interior regions; and the southeast coastal cultures, one of which has only recently returned to Alaska. Each group is different from other groups in many ways. They live in sometimes very different regions, they speak totally different languages, and they live very different lives in an often harsh environment. But these people have adapted their cultures to survive in Alaska, and they have done so for thousands of years.

Inuit

The Inuit (Eskimo) people of Alaska are divided into four groups based mostly upon their languages: Alutiiq, Central Yupik, Siberian Yupik, and Inupiaq. Anthropologists believe that Inuit first settled in Alaska about forty-five hundred years ago. They hunted seals, walrus, whales, and caribou, which abound in the Arctic and polar regions. The Inuit were not contacted by non-Natives until around 1780 in the southern regions and not until about 1850 in the northern regions. At that time, it was estimated that there were about thirty thousand to thirty-five thousand Inuit people living in Alaska. Today, about that same number of Inuit still live in Alaska. However, only about eighteen thousand people speak the traditional languages.

While most people tend to think that the Inuit lived in dome-shaped ice houses, they did not. Sometimes, while on hunting expeditions and trapped by severe weather, they might have carved houses from ice, but these were certainly not their regular homes. Instead, their permanent homes were semisubterranean—that is, half underground—with sod blocks cut from the tundra topsoil covering the

Aleut

The Aleut people traditionally lived on the Aleutian Islands, a nearly 1,000-mile (1,610-kilometer) chain of islands stretching far out into the Pacific Ocean. Anthropologists believe that Aleuts may have moved into the area as long as seven thousand years ago. In 1741, when Danish explorer Vitus Bering first encountered them, there were as many as fifteen thousand to eighteen thousand Aleuts. Today, there are some two thousand Aleuts living in Alaska, and only about five hundred people speak their traditional language.

Aleut settlements were generally built in protected places along the shoreline, where good beaches, freshwater streams, and high viewpoints to spot marine mammals were located. For the most part, communities were built along the southern side of the Aleutians facing the Pacific Ocean, instead of toward the Bering Sea on the northern side.

The traditional Aleut house is called the barabara. These homes were built using either wooden or whalebone frames with sod blocks and grass to cover them. They were as much as forty feet (twelve meters) long and twenty to thirty feet (six to nine meters) wide. Like Inuit homes, they were lit and heated by seal oil lamps.

The western Aleuts used boats made of seal skin to hunt sea lions, seals, sea otters, and whales. The central and eastern Aleuts hunted caribou and fished for salmon, halibut, and cod. They also collected bird eggs to eat, as well as clams, sea urchins, seaweed, and berries.

Athabascan

In the interior regions of Alaska, rich with rivers, streams, and lakes, live the Athabascan Indians. Anthropologists believe that these interior Indians have lived in the area for as long as ten thousand to eleven thousand years. This group of Alaska

A Native Alaskan family poses for the camera in a photograph taken in 1904.

roof. They were quite capable of comfortably housing families of eight to ten people. These homes were lit and heated by seal oil lamps.

To better hunt bowhead whales, seals, and walrus, Inuit built umiaks and kayaks made from stretched seal skins over sturdy wooden frames. These boats were very light and fast on the water. Umiaks were fifteen to twenty feet (five to six meters) long and could hold several hunters at one time. Kayaks were smaller and designed for usually only one person at a time. To hunt caribou on land, Inuit built lightweight sleds to pull supplies across the frozen tundra. Dogs were not used to pull sleds until about five hundred years ago, so the dogsled is a relatively new invention.

Natives was the last group to be contacted by outsiders. Most of the thirteen Indian cultures were not encountered until about 1850 to 1860. At contact, it was estimated that there were only about ten thousand Alaskan Athabascans. Today, there are only about five thousand Athabascans in Alaska and only about sixteen hundred Natives speak their traditional languages: Ahtna, Tanaina, Tanana, Kutchin, Han, Koyukon, Holikachuk, Deg Hi'tan, Upper Kuskokwim, Tanacross, Upper Tanana, Dena'ina, and Eyak. Most of these languages are in serious danger of becoming extinct in the next ten to twenty years, and Eyak has already lost all but one of its Native speakers.

Interior Athabascans primarily hunted moose, caribou, small mammals, and furbearing animals such as beavers, muskrats, rabbits, and ground squirrels for food and clothing material. They also relied a great deal on waterfowl and fish, including salmon, whitefish, pike, and burbot, as well as other freshwater species. Much of the time, these people had to migrate with the seasons to summer and winter camps.

Athabascans used birch-bark canoes to travel and hunt on rivers, lakes, and ponds. Upland Indians such as the Ahtna were highly skilled at creating snowshoes to walk through the deep snows of winter. They used long fishnets to dip salmon from the interior rivers to which millions of salmon migrated each summer to spawn upriver in the small streams and lakes where they were born.

Athabascan homes were generally constructed of wooden frames with animal skins stretched over them. These homes were sometimes as large as fourteen feet (four meters) across. In the winter, when temperatures sometimes dropped to as low as -60°F (-51°C), spruce tree boughs were placed over the house to insulate it from the cold.

One of the most important events in Indian life was the potlatch, a formal occasion when Natives gathered from distant but related villages, most often to celebrate deaths, but also at times to celebrate births, marriages, and a boy's first successful hunt. At these events, close relatives presented large quantities of blankets, items of wealth, and food to invited guests attending the ceremony.

Clothing made out of a variety of materials, including fur, wool, leather, and cotton, suits this Inuit family on a relatively mild Alaska day.

Inuit women from the Native village of Kotzebue, in Kotzebue, Alaska. Kotzebue is one of numerous bands that are organized into Native corporations that function in a way that is similar to reservations in the lower forty-eight U.S. states and to reserves in Canada.

Southeast Coastal Indians

Along the southeast coastline of Alaska lived the Tlingit, Haida, and Tsimshian peoples. Anthropologists believe that Tlingits may have settled in the area as long as two thousand to four thousand years ago. When they were first contacted by non-Natives around 1775 to 1800, there were as many as fifteen thousand Tlingits in Alaska. Today, there are about nine thousand Tlingits, and only about one thousand people speak the traditional language. The Haidas are recent newcomers to the area. It was only about four hundred years ago that Kaigani Haidas moved into the region of Alaska that they currently occupy. The Tsimshians moved into Alaska in 1887 from British Columbia.

Since they mostly lived in communities along the shoreline, most Tlingits and Haidas fished for their food, especially from the large runs of spawning salmon. They also fished for halibut, cod, and various rockfish, as well as for migrating eulachon, or candlefish, in the spring. Two of their most highly prized foods were dried salmon and herring eggs. Seals were also hunted, and seaweed and bird eggs were collected for food. Clams were readily available during low tides and were collected in the winter months.

From the mainland, moose, deer, and mountain goat were also hunted in the fall. Black bear and brown bear were occasionally hunted.

Tlingits and Haidas used two kinds of boats. One was a small ten- to sixteen-foot (three- to five-meter) cedar dugout for local hunting and fishing trips carrying no more than five or six people. The other kind of boat was also carved from cedar, but it was as much as twenty to fifty feet (six to fifteen meters) long. These boats, which were often decorated and painted on the sides, were used for long-distance travel, trade, and especially for warfare.

Tlingit and Haida homes were unlike those of any other Alaska Native group. Their homes were made with cedar planks and were as large as forty feet by sixty feet (twelve meters by eighteen meters), although the average home was smaller. These homes were painted with the totem symbol of the clan, usually an animal or fish. Large carved cedar poles, called totem poles, stood around the villages and in front of houses.

A group of Inuit children from the King Island Native Community at Nome, Alaska.

As with the Athabascan Indians of the interior, Tlingits and Haidas also had the potlatch ceremony. These events were even more lavish than those of the interior Indians.

Religion

Alaska Native peoples had different beliefs about the world around them, and, like most other cultures throughout the world, they had stories that embodied their beliefs. These stories, which often involved supernatural characters with magical powers and abilities, were different from one Native group to the next, but they shared some things in common.

They were all told to teach the young about the natural world around them, such as how things came to be as they currently are. These tales could also be used to teach people about the history of the people or the family or to teach how to act in their culture and how their customs came to be. Perhaps most important, these stories taught language.

The character most often used in stories is Raven, who is sometimes good but is usually greedy and selfish. In any event, however, he is always hungry. In many stories, he brings light and fire to the world. There are many stories, and no one knows how many there were because so many of the tales have been lost. Very few Natives still speak the traditional languages in which these stories were originally told.

Alaska Natives Today

There are many problems facing the Native people of Alaska today. Alaska Native communities and villages suffer from a lack of good sanitation and drinking water, from alcoholism, and from suicide rates much higher than the United States' national average. More than one-fourth of all Alaska Natives live in poverty, not having enough money to buy many items that most Americans already have.

Since hunting and fishing are still very important to rural Natives, their right to be allowed to continue to hunt and fish is also very important to them. More and more, the government is placing restrictions on these activities so that commercial fisherman especially can catch more fish such as salmon. Native leaders are trying to convince the government to allow them to continue hunting and fishing as they have done for thousands of years. In fact, some Native villages are trying to become sovereign, asking that they be allowed to govern their own affairs.

While as many as thirty thousand Alaska Natives live in Alaskan cities such as Anchorage, Fairbanks, Juneau, and Sitka, nearly fifty-six thousand still live in rural village communities and practice traditional subsistence lifestyles. In the past twenty years, there has been a revival of interest in preserving Alaska Native cultures and languages. Native languages are being taught in public schools, although up until only thirty years ago, they were severely discouraged in schools. Native arts are being produced and passed on to the younger generations.

— J. E. Smelcer

SEE ALSO:
Alaska; Alaska Native Claims Settlement Act (ANCSA); Aleut; Beringia; Giveaway; Haida; Inuit.

SUGGESTED READINGS:
Krauss, Michael E. *Native Peoples and Languages of Alaska* (map). Fairbanks: Alaska Native Language Center, 1982.
Langdon, Steve J. *The Native People of Alaska*. Anchorage, AK: Greatland Graphics, 1987.
Morgan, Lael, ed. *Alaska's Native People*. Anchorage: Alaska Geographic, 1979.
Smelcer, John E., ed. *The Raven and the Totem*. Anchorage, AK: Salmon Run, 1992.
———. *A Cycle of Myths*. Anchorage, AK: Salmon Run, 1993.

ALASKA NATIVE CLAIMS SETTLEMENT ACT (ANCSA)

One of the most important legislative acts of this century involving American Indians is the Alaska Native Claims Settlement Act of 1971. From around 1965 to 1971, the Alaska Federation of Natives (AFN), a delegation of people from every Native group of Alaska, lobbied the United States government for passage of a bill that would give land to Alaska Natives.

In their efforts to have Congress pass such a bill, AFN said that land was more important than money and asked the government for sixty million acres (twenty-four million hectares) of land and $500 million. It also requested a small percentage of money from State of Alaska resource revenues, such as money earned from the sale of oil from northern Alaska oil fields, some of the richest in the world. Such a settlement, it was believed, would protect Alaska Natives' rights to land use (including hunting and fishing), preserve their different cultures, and bring Indian self-government to Alaska Natives.

While most Native tribes in all other states had Indian reservations because of treaties signed before the twentieth century, Alaska Natives do not live on reservations. The leaders of AFN supported the idea of forming corporations, just like businesses, instead of creating and establishing Indian reservations. Thirteen regional Native corporations would be created to represent the various Native peoples of Alaska and their descendants. These corporations would manage land resources (such as timber and minerals) and authorize projects to promote the health, welfare, education, and general social well-being of their shareholders, the Native people who belonged to the corporations. The thirteen Native corporations that were to be formed are Ahtna Native Corporation, Inc.; Aleut Corporation; Arctic Slope Corporation; Bering Straits Corporation; Bristol Bay Corporation; Calista Corporation; Chugach Alaska Corporation; Cook Inlet Regional, Inc.; Doyon, Ltd.; Koniag, Inc.; NANA Regional Corporation; Sealaska Corporation; and the Thirteenth Regional Corporation.

After years of trying to get such a bill passed, Congress approved a bill that included giving $962,500,000 (nearly one billion dollars) and forty million acres (sixteen million hectares) of land—larger than several other states combined—to settle Alaskan Native claims. President Richard M. Nixon agreed to sign the bill only after AFN delegates met and approved the terms of the settlement.

At the president's invitation, the Alaska Federation of Natives met in Anchorage on December 18, 1971, at Alaska Pacific University, then called Alaska Methodist University, and voted on the legislation that was approved by the United States Congress. The AFN delegates voted to accept this legislation; President Nixon signed the bill into law, which has become known as ANCSA, or the Alaska Native Claims Settlement Act of 1971.

SEE ALSO:
Alaska; Alaska Natives.

ALBANY PLAN OF UNION (1754)

Nearly two generations before the Revolutionary War, leaders of the English colonies and the Iroquois Confederacy met to discuss the politics of alliance. Beginning in the early 1740s, Iroquois leaders strongly urged the colonists to form a federation similar to their own. The Iroquois' immediate practical objective was unified management of the Indian trade and preventing fraud, but they also stressed that the colonies should unify against France.

This set of circumstances brought Benjamin Franklin into the diplomatic equation. He first read the Iroquois' urgings to unite when he was a printer of Indian treaties. By the early 1750s, Franklin was more directly involved in diplomacy itself; at the same time, he became an early forceful advocate of colonial union. All of these circumstantial strings were tied together in the summer of 1754 when colonial representatives, Franklin among them, met with Iroquois sachems (leaders) at Albany, New York, to address issues of mutual concern and to develop the Albany Plan of Union, which echoes both English and Iroquois plans.

The Albany congress convened on June 19, 1754. Most of the sessions of the congress took place at the Albany courthouse. On June 28, 1754, the day after Mohawk leader Hendrick arrived with the Mohawk delegation, New York Governor James DeLancey met with him. The two hundred Indians in attendance sat on ten rows of benches in front of the governor's residence, with colonial delegates facing them in a row of chairs, their backs to the building. Hendrick repeated the advice that the Onondaga leader Canassatego had given colonial delegates a decade earlier: to unite according to the Iroquois model. This time, the advice came not at a treaty conference, but at a meeting devoted to drawing up a plan for the type of colonial union the Iroquois had been requesting. The same day, at the courthouse, the colonial delegates were in the early stages of debate over the plan of union.

DeLancey replied to Hendrick's advice that the colonists unite as the Iroquois had, "I hope that by this present Union, we shall grow up to a great height and be as powerful and famous as you were of old." The next day, July 10, 1754, Franklin formally proposed his plan of union before the Congress. Franklin wrote that the debates on the Albany Plan ". . . went on daily, hand in hand with the Indian business."

In drawing up his final draft, Franklin was meeting several diplomatic demands: the British monarchy's demand for control; the colonies' desires for autonomy in a loose confederation; and the Iroquois' stated advocacy for a colonial union similar (but not identical) to their own in form and function. Basically, the plan provided that the British parliament was to establish a general government in America, including all of the thirteen colonies, each of which was to retain its own constitution except for certain powers (mainly mutual defense) that were to be given to the general government. The king was to appoint a president-general for the government. Each colonial assembly would elect representatives to the grand council.

Franklin chose the name "Grand Council" for the plan's deliberative body, the same name generally applied to the Iroquois Central Council. The number of delegates, forty-eight, was close to the Iroquois council's fifty, and each colony had a different number of delegates, just as each Haudenosaunee (Iroquois) Nation sent a different number of sachems to Onondaga, the central meeting place for the Iroquois Confederacy. The retention of internal sovereignty within the individual colonies closely resembled the Iroquois system. The Albany Plan was based in rough proportion to tax revenues, however, while the Iroquois system was based on tradition.

The Albany plan was defeated by the colonies' individual assemblies, but it provided a model for Franklin's Articles of Confederation twenty years later.

SEE ALSO:
American Revolution; Canassatego; Franklin, Benjamin; Hendrick (Tiyanoga); Iroquois Confederacy.

ALBERTA

The westernmost prairie province of Canada, Alberta is also the fourth-largest province in the nation, with an area of about 252,000 square miles (655,200 square kilometers), including 6,490 square miles (16,874 square kilometers) of inland water. According to the 1986 Canadian census report, Alberta is the fourth most populous province, with 2,375,278 people. Alberta has ninety-six reserves, eight of which are Métis settlements. Those reserves covered by the Indian Act include 1,622,434 acres (656,856 hectares). Population counts of Native people living in Alberta vary. By one count, in 1989, Alberta had 57,590 status Indians (that is, members of tribes recognized by the Canadian government). Of that number, 34,782 lived on reserves. Recent census data records roughly 44,400 Natives, with about 25,000 living on reserves. In addition, Alberta's Métis population (those of mixed Native and French descent) ranges from about 27,000 to 60,000.

Major language groups in Alberta include the Algonquian and Athabascan languages. The Blackfeet, Bloods, and Piegan Indians (three of four tribes in the Blackfeet Confederacy) have lived for thousands of years in Alberta. Similarly, the Chipewyans have resided in Alberta's northern forests since time immemorial. In the 1600s, the Assiniboines made their way north from the Sioux (Dakota) tribes in Minnesota. About the same time, the Crees, as a result of contact with the Hudson's Bay Company, arrived in Alberta.

Between 1876 and 1899, Indians signed three treaties that covered such tribes as the Dene, Beaver, Cree, Chipewyan, and Sekani Nations; only the Lubicons never signed a treaty. The federal government reserved the right to interpret these treaties, always in favor of the settlers and developers who came west. When Alberta became a province, it also became an active participant in the interpretation of treaties, particularly in the areas of hunting, fishing, logging, and mining. Coupled with the near destruction of the buffalo and the establishment of residential schools, this had a devastating effect upon Native peoples.

Rich in fuel resources, Alberta produces about 80 percent of Canada's petroleum. Oil and gas revenues from some two hundred oil and gas wells go to seven Alberta bands. Despite these revenues, however, hunting, fishing, and trapping rights continue to be a source of disagreement between the various Indian bands and the two levels of Canadian government—provincial and federal. In addition, eleven bands have outstanding treaty land-entitlement claims, with five other bands having claims regarding the legality of government appropriation of land and the surrender of Native rights.

Indians were given the right to vote in federal elections in 1959 and the right to vote in provincial elections in 1965. For both on- and off-reserve, the largest occupations include service occupations and fishing, logging, mining, construction, professional, and clerical jobs. But unemployment rates among both status Natives and Métis are well above the national average, often ranging up to 60 percent unemployment within given communities.

In addition to its abundant natural resources, the province is also known for its wheat growing and cattle ranching. The land is dominated by green rolling hills and fertile plains. Sweet grass is abundant. Traditionally important to Native people, this sweet grass is picked and braided throughout the summer.

In 1989, the Métis Betterment Act gave the Métis title to 1,264,640 acres (512,000 hectares), limited self-government, and a $310 million cash settlement to be disbursed over a seventeen-year period. In 1990, most of Alberta's Métis population lived in urban settings such as Calgary and Edmonton.

A member of the Stoilo Nation in Alberta participates in a grass dance at the Casa Grande Powwow.

Cross-cultural awareness is currently of major concern to Canada's Natives. Aimed at bridging the cultural gap, sixteen Native Friendship Centres have been created across Alberta. These provide a variety of services, including social assistance and activities, financial assistance, and funds. Business services, educational programs, and counseling are also offered. Maintaining and developing Alberta's diverse Native culture is also a major focus for Friendship Centres. The cultural department of SIK-OOH-KOTOKI Friendship Society, Lethbridge, focuses on the Blackfeet syllabarium. The syllabarium is a systematic method of reproducing the phonetics of the Blackfeet language in script.

Writing-On-Stone Provincial Park, one of Alberta's tourist spots, preserves North America's most extensive collection of petroglyphs and pictographs. The major Native cultural site is Head-Smashed-In Buffalo Jump Interpretive Centre. It was designated a World Heritage Site by UNESCO (United Nations Educational, Scientific, and Cultural Organization). The Alberta Science Centre/Centennial Planetarium in Calgary presents another view of Native culture. Its "Skies of the Blackfoot Nations" planetarium production presents two Blackfeet sky legends.

— J. Arteno / G. William

SEE ALSO:
Algonquian; Assiniboine; Blackfeet; Canada, Native–Non-Native Relations in; Hudson's Bay Company; Métis.

ALCATRAZ ISLAND, OCCUPATION OF (1969)

Alcatraz Island, located off the San Francisco Bay, has been owned by the United States government since 1850. Known as the prison from which no one could escape, it was used as a federal penitentiary until it was abandoned in 1963.

A small band of Sioux who had been relocated to the San Francisco area landed on and claimed possession of the island in 1964. United States marshals expelled them a day later, and the group filed a suit in federal court. They cited Article 6 of an 1868 Sioux treaty that they claimed gave them the right to occupy and seek eventual ownership of federal land that is not mineral land or reserved by the United States for special purposes other than Native occupation.

The federal court dismissed the case, but attention to the long-forgotten treaties was not so easily dismissed. On November 20, 1969, a group of about eighty Native Americans, who called them-

Alcatraz Island, formerly a federal prison, adorned with emblems of the group known as Indians of All Tribes. American Indian activists occupied the island in an effort to develop a Native cultural center.

selves Indians of All Tribes (IAT), occupied the island and demanded the title to Alcatraz under the provision of an act passed on July 31, 1882. The act indicated that abandoned federal facilities should be used for Indian schools. The Indian occupants mounted tipis and stated they were enjoying all the comforts of home on the reservations.

IAT, led by Richard Oaks (Mohawk) and John Trudell (Santee Dakota), stated it wanted to use Alcatraz Island for an educational, cultural, and spiritual center. They asked that a center for Native American Studies, an American Indian Spiritual Center, an Indian Center of Ecology, a Great Indian Training School, and an American Indian Museum be established. Though IAT pointed out that the original Native owners had never ceded the island, the occupants offered to buy the island for twenty-four dollars in glass beads and red cloth, a precedent set by the sale of Manhattan Island in 1626.

Another part of the group's agenda was to publicize the desperate conditions of American Indians. A statement released by IAT declared: "We feel that this so-called Alcatraz Island is more suitable for an Indian Reservation, as determined by the white man's own standard. By this we mean that this place resembles most Indian reservations in that:

"1. It is isolated from modern facilities, and without adequate means of transportation.

"2. It has no fresh running water.

"3. It has inadequate sanitation facilities.

"4. There are no oil or mineral rights.

"5. There is no industry, and so unemployment is very great.

Indian Alcatraz leaders *(left to right)* Richard Oakes, Earl Livermore, and Al Miller meet with the press on December 24, 1969, to discuss their objectives, which include drawing attention to the plight of Indians living on reservations.

"6. There are no health care facilities.

"7. The soil is rocky and unproductive, and the land does not support game.

"8. There are no educational facilities.

"9. The population has always exceeded the land base.

"10. The population has always been held as prisoners and kept dependent on others.

"Further," declared IAT, "it would be fitting and symbolic that ships from all over the world, entering the Golden Gate, would first see Indian land,

and thus be reminded of the true history of this nation. This tiny island would be a symbol of the great lands once ruled by free and noble Indians."

The occupants resolved, "We must forever survive as Indians." To this end, John Trudell traveled throughout the United States, raising support for the return of Alcatraz Island to the Natives. He also became the voice of Radio Free Alcatraz, a program explaining Native issues to the rest of the United States.

Church groups and sympathizers arranged for food and medical supplies to be shipped to the island during the occupation. Reporters visited the island and came back to the mainland with stories of the Natives' search for true self-determination and the horrible conditions of reservation life throughout the United States.

In December, Congress passed a joint resolution requiring the president "to initiate immediate negotiations with delegated representatives of IAT and other appropriate representatives of the Indian community." President Richard Nixon dispatched Robert Robertson, executive director of the Nation Council of Indian Opportunity, to Alcatraz. Robertson asked that the women and children be immediately removed and the IAT contingent be reduced to a "symbolic force" of five to ten men to be placed on the federal payroll. This would be the requirements for further discussions. The group refused.

The Department of the Interior then offered to make Alcatraz a national park with the theme of "Indian quality" and hire Natives as park rangers and to serve on the facility's planning board. Again—on March 3, 1970—IAT refused the idea.

In May, the United States Coast Guard was ordered to deny electricity to the Indians occupying the island. Also, the barge used to take supplies to the island was taken out of service. IAT reduced its force and prepared for a serious siege.

On June 14, about twenty U.S. marshals armed with shotguns and automatic weapons landed on the island. Only about fifteen Natives were on the island at the time as the others were either shopping for supplies or working somewhere to buy the supplies needed. The IAT members on the island were removed at gunpoint, taken to nearby Treasure Island, and eventually released.

Although the siege was over, Alcatraz Island became a symbol of freedom to many Native Americans, on and off reservations. Those who took part in the occupation remember it as a beautiful experience and as a symbol of the Natives' need to retake the continent, at least in spirit.

The occupation brought Indians from throughout the country to participate in the Alcatraz experience and share in the act of rebellion. At one point, almost one thousand Native Americans were staying on the island. The occupation became a "declaration of independence" for Native people and a symbol of the renewed quest for freedom.

Other occupations and demonstrations followed but were only noticed as long as the mass media found them interesting. The occupation of Alcatraz stirred Native hearts and was a catalyst for later events, including marches, demonstrations, and occupations, that brought about change and a new awareness of the condition of Indian America.

— S. S. Davis

SEE ALSO:

American Indian Movement; Pine Ridge Reservation, Conflict at; Trail of Broken Treaties; Trudell, John; Wounded Knee, Confrontation at (1973).

ALCOHOLISM

Various economic, health, and social problems have long plagued Native American societies, but possibly the most destructive and serious issue facing Indian communities today is the problem of alcohol abuse and the many related hazards it creates. Alcoholism's most telling impact on Indian communities lies in the death statistics. Alcohol-related deaths occurring from suicides, auto accidents, homicides, and cirrhosis of the liver affect an alarmingly greater proportion of Native people than non-Natives. While the average life expectancy for Americans as a whole has climbed steadily—among some groups, it is well into the seventies—Native American life expectancy is only around fifty years of age. Perhaps over three-fourths of Native American suicide cases are alcohol related, and nearly all crimes for which Native Americans are imprisoned are committed while the individual is under the influence of alcohol.

It is also of great concern that Native Americans die from alcohol-related diseases at four times the national rate. The occurrence of Fetal Alcohol Syndrome (FAS) and Fetal Alcohol Effect (FAE) is over thirty times higher in the Native American population than in the Anglo-American population. Numbers like these have effects that go beyond the medical and psychological problems associated with alcohol and into the fabric of Indian societies. For example, the high school dropout rate among Native Americans—the highest of any minority group—is related to alcohol abuse among Indian teens.

Much of the reason for the high percentage of alcohol abuse among Native American people lies in the fact that the poverty rate for Indian families is more than twice the rate of the general population. Reservations are known for chronic poverty and deprivation, and fewer than 30 percent of Native Americans from the ages of sixteen to sixty-four on reservations earn more than seven thousand dollars a year. Living among extreme poverty brings about feelings of low self-esteem and desolation, which makes some Native people highly susceptible to the abuse of alcohol and other substances as a means of escaping from the seemingly hopeless reality of reservation life.

Along with firearms, metal tools, coffee, and other useful products that Europeans brought to Native American people for trade, liquor was among the "goods." Alcohol was originally a diplomatic device between European-Americans and Native Americans, used frequently to steer negotiations in favor of the European-Americans.

In later centuries, though laws forbade the frontiersmen, traders, and settlers to give liquor to Native Americans, many continued to do so. A trader could obtain a valuable buffalo robe from an Indian for just a small amount of liquor, and soon alcohol became a cheap and profitable form of merchandise. Traders were known to often dilute whiskey until it contained mostly water, mixed with pepper, gunpowder, and tobacco to give it a "kick." In the earliest times, Native Americans did not care for the strong taste of alcohol, which was in the form of whiskey, but they grew to use the intoxicants through the persistent offerings by explorers who wanted to show their friendship by making the Indians they encountered "feel good."

Alcoholism was thus destined to become yet another of the many tragic diseases Europeans brought to North America that Native people were not equipped to handle. The disease took its place among smallpox, tuberculosis, measles, cholera, and others. Some studies indicate that types of alcohol abuse, such as binge drinking patterns, are learned behaviors. Native Americans adopted the "frontier-style" drinking habits of the trappers, prospectors, soldiers, and frontier adventurers, who themselves were often hard binge drinkers. Today, the "frontier-style" survives on many reservations, as it does among various non-Native groups living in remote communities, western cowboy towns, northwestern coastal fishing villages, and Alaskan boomtowns.

Many recent studies have shown that popular conceptions of the stereotypical "drunken Indian" or the general assumption that Native Americans as a race or ethnic group have a genetic weakness toward alcohol are false. No scientific evidence has been found that implies that Native Americans might metabolize alcohol any more slowly or quickly than people of other races or that Native Americans carry a gene that compels them to abuse alcohol. But still, many of these myths persist, even among Native American people themselves.

To further compound the alcohol problem, beer companies are known to traditionally target Native American reservations with advertising campaigns. Beer distributors near tribal lands have been involved with funding American Indian celebrations or annual events, displaying banners and company trademark mementos. Beer mascots are known to distribute miniature rolls of candy packaged as tiny beer cans, targeting young people. These types of advertising campaigns send the wrong message to Native youth. Though abuse of other kinds of drugs like marijuana or cocaine is prevalent among reservation youth, alcohol abuse still remains the most serious problem.

In 1832, Congress passed legislation prohibiting the sale of liquor to Indian people, and in 1953, the law was repealed, leaving the decision to the tribal governments. Since the repeal, reservations that were previously "dry" became faced with the new threat of alcohol abuse and its many related problems. Through tribal sovereignty laws, many United States reservations have enforced prohibition of the sale of alcohol; however, about 35 percent of the nation's three hundred reservations allow the sale and consumption of alcohol. While the prohibition of alcohol on reservations is thought to lessen abuse and diminish its related problems, studies have found that very often this isn't the case. Alcoholism still remains a main concern, even on dry reservations.

Alcoholism has taken a heavy toll among Native American communities, but through ongoing health and educational programs to promote abstinence, many communities have made great strides in fighting the disease.

— T. Midge

SEE ALSO:
AIDS; Epidemic Diseases; Fetal Alcohol Syndrome; "Firewater."

SUGGESTED READINGS:
Dorris, Michael. *The Broken Cord*. New York: Harper-Collins Publishers, 1989.
Erdoes, Richard. *The Sun Dance People*. New York: Alfred A. Knopf, 1972.
Jones, Jayne Clark. *The American Indian in America*. Minnesota: Lerner Publications, 1973.
Leland, Joy. *Firewater Myths*. New Brunswick, NJ: Rutgers Center of Alcohol Studies, 1976.
Nabokov, Peter. *Native American Testimony*. New York: Viking, 1991.
Olson, James S., and Raymond Wilson. *Native Americans in the Twentieth Century*. Chicago: University of Illinois Press, 1986.
Rausch, David A., and Blair Schlepp. *Native American Voices*. Grand Rapids, MI: Baker Books, 1994.

ALEUT

The Aleuts are the Native inhabitants of the seventy Aleutian Islands that stretch for about 1,000 miles (1,610 kilometers) southwest off the Alaskan mainland. Today, these islands are part of the U.S. state of Alaska. A small number of Aleuts also occupy a narrow strip of land along the western Alaskan coastline. It was the Russians who first called these maritime hunters "Aleuts," although the meaning of this term is unknown; the Aleuts call themselves *Unangan*, meaning "The People."

The Aleut Way of Life
The Aleuts had to adapt to a harsh, wet ocean climate with great temperature extremes, high winds, and much dense fog. Sudden and violent windstorms called williwaws, powerful enough to uproot houses and smash fishing boats, often unleashed solid walls of water that wiped out whole communities. Yet Aleuts were convinced their islands were the world's best place to live.

Their skill at hunting sea mammals ensured a bountiful supply of food. This type of hunting required patience, finely crafted weapons, and a great deal of skill. Men trained for this activity from the time they were young children with special exercises to strengthen their endurance and lengthen their arm ligaments to make them better harpooners. Aleut hunters stalked whales, otters, sea lions, and seals from their flexible boats—light, skin-covered, one- or two-person kayaks. They used harpoons and throwing boards attached to ropes to first spear their prey and then drag it into the boat, where they could kill it with a club. Hunters with clubs also stalked seals on land.

Aleuts used these sea mammals for more than food. They depended on the skins, flippers, and intestines for waterproof clothing and boats, on the oil to light their lamps, and on the bones to make weapons and tools. While men hunted sea mammals or fished, women and children collected shellfish and octopuses from the shallow beach areas and set out snares to catch puffins.

Aleuts lived in villages that were so well camouflaged that a visitor to the islands could have easily overlooked them. An entire village of two hundred or more Aleuts could be contained in five large subterranean houses called barabaras. Split timbers, planks, and sometimes whalebones were sunk into deep holes dug into hillsides, then covered over with sod and thatched grass so that they blended into the green hills. A hatch was built into the center of the roof to let in light. It also served as an outlet for smoke and provided the only way to enter or exit the house. Cooking was generally done on hearths outside the house.

Each house was made up of cubicles or compartments that were inhabited by individual family groups, usually grandparents, parents, and their children. There were no village leaders, only headmen of households—usually the most able-bodied male in a multifamily house. As a result, villages usually had as many headmen as there were households. These headmen led hunting and fishing parties and presided over certain ceremonies.

Each village maintained a scanning system in which residents took turns watching the land and surrounding sea for sudden bad weather, whale sightings, communications from neighboring villages, and any other noteworthy signs. Visits between villages were major social events and usually featured dancing, singing, storytelling, and wrestling contests. These public contests also functioned as ways to settle feuds and resolve bad feelings between villages without resorting to warfare, which was rare among the Aleuts.

In summer, households usually broke up into smaller family units that traveled inland to salmon streams and other areas where they could collect berries, eggs, roots, and various birds not found along the coast. These smaller family units often set up improvised tents on these trips, sometimes creating small temporary villages in the process.

An Aleut family photographed in August 1942. Perhaps in an effort to arouse patriotic impulses in Americans during World War II, the news release accompanying this photo speculated that the family may have been taken prisoner by Japanese patrols invading the islands, which jut out toward Asia from the Alaskan (and thus U.S.) mainland.

Aleut Art and Religion

Aleut men had many types of knives, awls, fishing hooks, harpoons, and other hunting tools for which they carved wooden, soapstone, or whalebone handles in the shapes of animal spirits. Men also wore conical wooden ceremonial hats, which they decorated with paintings and ivory figures. Women wove cloth, made blankets, and created expertly sewn clothing, which they decorated with paint, feathers, and leather tooling. Both men and women wore carved bone, ivory, and feather jewelry that pierced their earlobes, noses, and lower lips. Tattoos on the face and hands were also common. Many Aleut people liked to dance and sing and were enthusiastic storytellers.

The Aleuts believed that all life-forms had spirits and that human souls were often reincarnated after death in newborn babies. They always made

An undated engraving of an Aleut couple holding an oar against a backdrop that includes a coastline and several kayaks.

When they brought back stories of plentiful sea otter, seal, and blue fox pelts, Russian fur traders immediately set sail for the Aleutians, eager to make their fortunes. The Aleut name for these Russians was *Cossack,* taken from the military rank of one of the first explorers they encountered. Because the Russians wanted the pelts but had neither the hunting expertise nor the ability to adapt to the harsh climate, they tried convincing the Aleuts to hunt for them. But the Aleuts had no interest in collecting pelts for the Russians. Hostilities broke out almost immediately and continued throughout the long Russian occupation of the islands. The Aleuts resisted valiantly, but those the Russians couldn't shoot, they starved into submission. As a result, the original population of the Aleuts—over sixteen thousand people—was reduced by almost one-half in the first forty years of Russian contact. They never recovered.

In spite of this mistreatment, the Aleuts quickly learned Russian and adopted many Russian customs, including advanced boat design, cloth sails, sleds, the use of needles and awls, kettles, axes, tobacco, tea, and steam baths. They even learned chess and quickly became masters at the game. The Russians, on the other hand, learned little about the Aleut culture, even though Aleut hunting and survival techniques could have profited them greatly.

Over the next hundred years, epidemic diseases, forced labor, and continuing hostilities further reduced the population until 1867, when the Russian government, financially devastated from fighting the Crimean War, negotiated to sell Alaska and the Aleutian Islands to the United States for $7.2 million. Fishing grew in importance after 1867,

sure to thank the spirits of animals through prayer and ritual before they killed them for food or clothing. Most villages had a shaman, a man or woman who had the power to diagnose and treat sickness and to call on appropriate spirits to protect the village or ensure a successful hunt.

Interaction with Russians and the United States

Russian explorers happened first upon Alaska and then the neighboring Aleutian Islands in 1741.

and, in 1878, the first salmon cannery was opened. Americans moved quickly to take charge of the profitable fur seal trade but otherwise neglected the region until 1910 after fur seals had been killed in such great numbers that the federal government had to take control of the herds to prevent the animals' extermination.

In 1942, the Japanese invaded and occupied several of the Aleutian Islands. The United States was able to retake these islands in 1943 and then used them as a strategic army base against Japan for the rest of the war. This military buildup, which carried over to the postwar period, helped create new economic development in the islands and encouraged other Americans to move there.

In 1959, after major oil fields discovered in Alaska created an important new petroleum industry, Congress approved statehood for Alaskan territory. This territory included the Aleutian Islands. Under additional national legislation passed in 1971, 44 million acres (17.6 million hectares) of federal land in the state was reserved for Alaska's Inuit and Aleut populations. (A federal court ruled in 1991 that these lands could be considered sovereign "Indian Country," even though they were not reservations.) Today, about eight thousand Aleuts live in the state of Alaska.

— P. Press

SEE ALSO:
Alaska; Alaska Natives; Inuit.

SUGGESTED READINGS:

Brody, Hugh. *Living Arctic, Hunters of the Canadian North.* Seattle: University of Washington Press, 1987.

Dumond, Don. E. *The Eskimos and Aleuts.* London: Thames and Hudson, 1987.

Driver, Harold Edson. *Indians of North America.* Chicago: University of Chicago Press, 1965.

Nabokov, Peter, ed. *Native American Testimony: A Chronicle of Indian-White Relations from Prophecy to the Present.* New York: Viking Penguin, 1991.

Utley, Robert M. *The Indian Frontier of the American West, 1846–1890.* Albuquerque: University of New Mexico Press, 1983.

ALEXIE, SHERMAN (1966–)

Sherman Alexie, a Spokane–Coeur d'Alene born in 1966, grew up in Wellpinit, Washington, on the Spokane Indian Reservation, which forms the backdrop for much of his writing. He is the author of four books of poetry, *The Business of Fancydancing* (Hanging Loose Press, 1992); *I Would Steal Horses* (Slipstream Press, 1992), which won the Fifth Annual Slipstream Chapbook Contest; *Old Shirts and New Skins* (UCLA American Indian Studies Center, University of California Press, 1993); and *First Indian on the Moon* (Hanging Loose Press, 1993). His fiction includes *The Lone Ranger and Tonto Fistfight in Heaven* (Atlantic Monthly Press, 1993) and *Reservation Blues* (Atlantic Monthly Press, 1995).

Alexie won poetry fellowships in 1991 from the Washington State Arts Commission and in

Writer and storyteller Sherman Alexie, photographed at the Indian Community House in New York City in 1994.

59

1992 from the National Endowment for the Arts. He is a citation winner of the PEN/Hemingway Award for best book of fiction and a winner of a 1994 Lila Wallace–*Reader's Digest* Award. His short stories have appeared in a number of publications, including *Esquire*, and in anthologies of Native American fiction, such as *Earth Song, Sky Spirit* (Doubleday, 1993). His poetry has appeared in many publications, including such anthologies as *Durable Breath* (Salmon Run Press, 1994) and *Returning the Gift* (University of Arizona Press, 1994).

In *The Business of Fancydancing*, Alexie's poetry is noteworthy for its honesty in depicting Indian life, its avoidance of romantic images, and its skillful use of humor. The book garnered Alexie a good deal of attention and a very favorable front-page review in *The New York Times Book Review*, which bolstered his career and created interest in his work. *The Lone Ranger and Tonto Fistfight in Heaven* is a collection of connected stories that some feel is actually a novel. Its central character, Victor, gives vivid accounts of reservation life, especially in his humorous observations. These observations show how humor can be a survival tool. *Reservation Blues* combines realism and magic in a novel that is both a bitter and comic tale centering on Coyote Springs, an all-Indian, Catholic rock 'n' roll band.

In much of his writing, Alexie's bitter, double-edged jokes give attention to the many forms oppression takes, yet they point to continuance and hope at the same time. Alexie is especially impressive as a public reader and is known for giving moving and hilarious oral performances of his stories from memory.

ALGONQUIAN

Algonquian (or *Algonkian*) is a name that has come to be associated with those Native American tribes whose languages can be traced back to one common language, Algonquian. In addition to language, the Algonquians also share a similar culture and similar social organizations. Some of the Algonquian-speaking tribes have at times formed loose confederations—for example, the Powhatan Confederacy—but most of the tribes live independently from each other.

Some scholars think that the Algonquians lived in Canada at one time, in the area north of the St. Lawrence River and east of Lake Ontario. From there, the Algonquian tribes are thought to have spread over a large part of North America. Occupying most of the land east of the Mississippi, they range from Labrador and Hudson Bay in the north to Tennessee and Virginia in the south.

The Crees, Micmacs, and Naskapis are found in Labrador and Nova Scotia. In New England are the Abenakis, Mahicans, Massachusetts, Mohegans, Narragansetts, Penobscots, Pequots, Poktumtuks, and Wampanoags. Along the Atlantic Coast are the Lenapes (Delawares), Nanticokes, and the Powhatan Confederacy. Near the Great Lakes are the Crees, Lenapes (Delawares), Illinois, Kickapoos, Menominees, Miamis, Ojibwes (Chippewas), Ottawas, Peorias, Potawatomis, Sac (Sauk) and Fox, and Shawnees. On the Great Plains are the Arapahos, Atsinas (Gros Ventres), Blackfeet (Bloods, Piegans, and Siksikas), Cheyennes, and Plains Crees.

At the time of European contact, some of the Algonquians lived in single dome-shaped oval houses called wigwams. Large pieces of bark or mats woven out of grass were placed over a frame of poles to form the walls. In the center of the wigwam was a fireplace. The floor was tamped earth, and platforms stretched around the wigwam's sides for sitting and sleeping. In summer, brush tents were also used for living. Other Algonquian tribes lived in communal longhouses. Palisades of stakes surrounded the villages.

Clothing typically consisted of moccasins, leggings, a breechcloth, and a robe for men. Women wore the so-called Algonquian slit skirt. It consisted of a rectangular piece of deerskin and fell just below the knee. The skin overlapped on the right side and was held with a belt. Sometimes women also wore a jacket.

Deer meat was the major food for members of the Algonquian tribes, with the exception of the Plains tribes, who hunted buffalo. Their meat diet was supplemented with such foods as corn, squash, and beans, grown by the women in fields and gardens. Tobacco, also cultivated, was used for cere-

A Lenape (Delaware) traditional dancer dressed in regalia. Living primarily in the northeastern part of the present-day United States (the Atlantic seaboard and Great Lakes), the Lenapes were one of several dozen Indian groups related primarily by the Algonquian language family. They were forced to relocate as far afield as Missouri, Oklahoma, and parts of Canada by the influx of European-Americans into their traditional lands.

monies. Many European colonizers adopted foods and recipes from the Algonquian people—for example, hominy, succotash, persimmon bread, popcorn, and maple sugar.

Tools were made of bark, wood, and stones. The Algonquian tribes fashioned baskets of wood splints and used black pottery with pointed bottoms. Woven bags, belts, and straps from thread made out of the inner bark of trees were also produced.

Traditional Algonquian stories tell of respect for light, in the form of the sun and fire, and for the four winds, represented by animals. All tribes believe in a communion of human beings and animals. Algonquians have a guardian spirit, a so-called totem, in the form of an animal or bird. Algonquian cultural heroes gave directions for living, taught laws and the arts, and supplied the people with corn and tobacco. Stories, songs, ceremonies, and a tribe's history were recorded on birch bark in a highly developed picture writing.

Algonquians were the first Indians to encounter the Europeans, who arrived on the northern Atlantic coast of North America. In Jamestown, Virginia, the Powhatans, under their leader Wahunsonacock (also known as Powhatan), helped the first English colonists to survive. It is said that Pocahontas, daughter of Wahunsonacock, rescued the leader of the colony, John Smith, from her father's anger and made possible peaceful relations between the tribes and the colonists. (The truth of this tale may lie somewhere beyond—or short of—the story that most people associate with Pocahontas; for example, some historians and others have suggested that the "rescue" of John Smith may have been part of a ritual initiation of Smith into the tribe.)

Further north, in Massachusetts, Squanto (Tisquantum), a Wampanoag, and Massasoit, chief of the Wampanoag, helped the Pilgrims survive their first year in Plymouth by showing them how to plant corn, how to hunt local game, and where to fish in the rivers. In the fall of 1621, the Wampanoags introduced the colonists to their annual celebration of giving thanks. A feast was held that lasted three days, during which both Wampanoags and European colonists gave thanks for a rich harvest.

Great leaders of Algonquian stock include King Philip (Metacom), who was a Wampanoag and the son of Massasoit. Together with his general Canonchet, a Narragansett, he tried to defend his homeland during the war of 1675 to 1676. Almost a hundred years later, Pontiac, an Ottawa, attempted to unite several tribes to resist the advancing colonizers. In 1811, Tecumseh, a Shawnee, sought to form a confederation for the same purpose. Black Hawk, a Sauk, also tried to unite Indians against encroachment in the Mississippi River Valley. Today, many prominent Indian leaders are from Algonquian tribes.

— H. Weidner

SEE ALSO:
Abenaki; Arapaho; Blackfeet; Black Hawk; Buffalo; Cheyenne; Gros Ventre; Illinois Confederacy; Kickapoo; King Philip's War; Lenape; Massachusetts; Massasoit; Menominee; Miami; Micmac; Narragansett; Ojibwe; Ottawa; Penobscot; Pequot; Pocahontas; Pontiac; Potawatomi; Sac and Fox; Shawnee; Squanto; Tecumseh; Wahunsonacock (Powhatan); Wampanoag; Wappinger; Wigwam.

SUGGESTED READINGS:
Josephy, Alvin M., Jr. *The Indian Heritage of America.* New York: Bantam Books, 1968.
Kroeber, A. L. *Cultural and Natural Areas of Native North America.* Berkeley: University of California Press, 1939.
Lincoln, Charles H., ed. *Narratives of the Indian Wars, 1675–1699.* New York: Barnes and Noble, 1952.
Owens, R. C., et al. *The North American Indians: A Sourcebook.* New York: Macmillan, 1967.
Ritzenthaler, Robert, and Pat Ritzenthaler. *The Woodland Indians of the Western Great Lakes.* Garden City, NY: Natural History Press, 1970.
Rogers, John (Snow Cloud). *Red World and White: Memories of a Chippewa Boyhood* (Published in 1957 as *A Chippewa Speaks*). Norman: University of Oklahoma Press, 1974.
Stevens, W. E. *The Northwest Fur Trade, 1763–1800.* Urbana: University of Illinois Press, 1928.
Vaughan, Alan T. *New England Frontier: Puritans and Indians, 1620–1675.* Boston: Little, Brown & Co., 1965.
Vlahos, Olivia. *New World Beginnings: Indian Culture in the Americas.* New York: Viking, 1970.

ALLEN, PAULA GUNN
(1939–)

Paula Gunn Allen, of Laguna Pueblo and Lebanese descent, was born in Cubero, New Mexico, in 1939. Her wide-ranging writing has included poetry, fiction, a novel, and critical studies, and she has taught at major universities, currently at the University of California at Los Angeles. Her poetry includes *The Blind Lion* (1974), *Coyote's Daylight Trip* (1978), *A Cannon Between My Knees* (1981), *Star Child* (1981), *Shadow Country* (1982), *Wyrds* (1987), and *Skins and Bones* (1988). Allen's novel, *The Woman Who Owned the Shadows*, deals with an urban Laguna woman learning to imagine her own identity apart from men. She draws upon her home landscape as she develops a feeling of inner strength and wholeness.

In addition to works of poetry and fiction, Allen has demonstrated insight as a literary and cultural critic. She has published a number of analytical essays and book-length works on Native American literature and the teaching of it. The book she edited, entitled *Studies in American Indian Literature: Critical Essays and Course Designs*, contains analyses of Native American novels and poetry, course descriptions, and strategies for teaching Native literature in the classroom. Her book, *The Sacred Hoop: Recovering the Feminine in American Indian Traditions*, combines feminism with tribal perspectives in a unique merging. In it, she argues that the roles of women in portrayals of American Indians have been minimized. In fact, all of her work demonstrates her commitment to women's issues. In another edited anthology of Native women writers, *Spider Woman's Granddaughters*, Gunn Allen offers a discussion of women's themes preceding each selection. In *Grandmothers of the Light: A Medicine Woman's Sourcebook*, she explores further women-centered cultures and spirit-based views of the universe.

SEE ALSO:
Pueblo.

Laguna writer Paula Gunn Allen, shown at an engagement in Brockport, New York, in 1996.

ALL INDIAN PUEBLO COUNCIL

The contemporary All Indian Pueblo Council had its origins in a meeting at Santo Domingo Pueblo on November 5, 1922. In 1922, the first chairman of the All Indian Pueblo Council was Sotero Ortiz, of San Juan Pueblo, and the first secretary was Pablo Abeita, of Isleta Pueblo. The purpose of the meeting was to organize Pueblo opposition to pending legislation, known as the Bursum Bill, which had been introduced in the United States Senate by Senator Holm O. Bursum of New Mexico. The bill, entitled An Act to Quit Title to Lands within Pueblo Indian Land Grants, would have allowed approximately twelve thousand non-Indian squatters on Pueblo land in New Mexico to secure title to the land they occupied. It also would have taken Pueblo water rights out of federal jurisdiction and

Sotero Ortiz, first chairman of the All Indian Pueblo Council, at a 1924 meeting of Native leaders over issues affecting Pueblo land and water rights.

Under the council's new constitution, each of the governments of the Indian pueblos in New Mexico can designate a delegate to the council to represent it. The council elects its officers every two years from among the delegates from the member pueblos. The council has the power: to represent its member pueblos by employing legal counsel; to negotiate with all governments, persons, firms, or corporations on matters brought before the council; to enter into contracts and accept loans or grants; to arrange for the maintenance of law and order at council functions; to promote educational, health, and other programs and projects for the general welfare of the member pueblos; to raise revenue for the business of the council; and "to do whatever else may be necessary or desirable to promote the general welfare of any or all member-pueblos." The council is also prohibited from interfering with the self-government of any member pueblo. Other articles of the constitution deal with the internal operations of the council, as well as provisions for amending the constitution and the ratification of the document. Since the adoption of the new constitution for the council, the Pueblos have continued to promote economic and educational opportunities and to seek unified action on issues regarding water rights, land rights, and the preservation of Pueblo cultural values.

According to the oral history of the Pueblos, something similar to the All Indian Pueblo Council has been in operation since before the arrival of Europeans on the continent. The logo of the All Indian Pueblo Council bears the date of 1598 to commemorate the first meeting of the council to appear in European historical records, when Juan de Oñate, the Spanish colonizer of New Mexico, met with thirty-eight Pueblo leaders at Santo Domingo Pueblo. Much of the activities of the council were conducted in secret during the Spanish colonial era, such as meetings to plan the Pueblo

placed their allocation with state officials who were unsympathetic with Pueblo agricultural needs. The bill had the support of the secretary of the interior, Albert B. Fall, who was from New Mexico, as well as the support of President Warren Harding's administration. Vigorous opposition by the Pueblos, through the All Indian Pueblo Council, succeeded in defeating the legislation.

On October 16, 1965, under the chairmanship of Domingo Montoya of Sandia Pueblo, a new constitution was adopted. Its preamble set forth some of the organization's goals: promoting justice, fostering social and economic advancement for all Pueblos, protecting common interests, preserving the right to tribal self-government, and preserving rights guaranteed by treaties, laws, and the U.S. Constitution.

A resident of the Santo Domingo Pueblo, a community with historic ties to the first recorded All Indian Pueblo Council meeting (in 1598) and to the origins of the present council (in 1922).

Revolt of 1680, which drove the Spanish out of New Mexico for twelve years.

The All Indian Pueblo Council logo was designed by Joe S. Sando, of Jemez Pueblo, in 1970, while he was serving as secretary of the council, and the logo was painted by Jerry Ingram, a Creek (Muscogee) from Oklahoma. The logo is a circle with the date 1598 flanking the sacred sun symbol, as the symbol stands above mountains, a river, and cultivated fields. A harvest of corn, wheat, chile, melons, and squash appears at the bottom, along with the inscription All Indian Pueblo Council.

— D. L. Birchfield

SEE ALSO:
Acoma Pueblo; Arizona; Isleta Pueblo; Kachina; New Mexico; New Spain; Oñate Expedition; Pueblo Revolt of 1680; Southwest Literature, Contemporary; Taos Pueblo; Tewa Pueblo; Tiwa Pueblo; Zuni.

AMERICA AND AMERICANS

The name *America* first began to appear on maps in the early 1500s, always being placed in the area of present-day Venezuela (in South America) or toward Nicaragua (in Central America). Later, the name was applied to the entire continent of America, consisting of North America, South America, the Caribbean Sea, and offshore areas such as Newfoundland and Greenland. Today, the plural form of *the Americas* is sometimes used because of the many subregions, such as North America, South America, Mesoamerica (Mexico and northern Central America), and Central America.

Some historians have theorized that *America* as a name may stem from the mountain range known as Amerique located in Nicaragua, or it may stem from a word common to several Native American languages of the Caribbean and South America, namely *maraca*. This word may be pro-

Evidence suggests that various Native names, combined with their treatment by early Spanish explorers, may have had more to do with the naming of America than this man, Amerigo Vespucci, who was actually better known in his own day as Albérico.

nounced in several ways. In one, the emphasis is on the second syllable—*maráca*. In another, it is on the first syllable—*máraca*—which would give the word a sound similar to *america*. Maraca, meaning rattle or gourd, is found as a place name in Venezuela (Maracapana, Maracay, Maracaibo), in Trinidad (Maracas), in Puerto Rico (Maracayu), in Brazil (Maraca, Itamaraca), and elsewhere.

Many very early maps of the Caribbean region show an island located to the northwest of Venezuela (where Nicaragua is actually located) called "Tamaraque," which has been interpreted as "T. Amaraque," standing for "tierra" or "terra (land) of Amaraque."

Most of us have probably been taught that America as a name is derived from that of Amerigo Vespucci. Strangely enough, Vespucci's first name is more often recorded as Albérico rather than Amerigo. It may well be that the name *America* is not derived from his name, but we know for sure that it was first applied to South America or Central America and *not* to the area of the United States.

From the early 1500s until the mid-1700s, the only people called Americans were those who were indigenous to the continent—the ancestors of the people who are today called Native American, American Indian, or First Nations people. Similarly, the people called Mexicans, Canadians, Brazilians, Peruvians, and so on, were all Native people. In 1578, for example, George Best of Britain wrote about "those Americans and Indians"—a reference to our Native American ancestors as Americans and the people of India and Indonesia as Indians. In 1650, a Dutch work referred to the Algonquians of the Manhattan area as "the Americans or Natives." In 1771, a Dutch dictionary noted that "the Americans are red in their skins." As late as 1845, another Dutch dictionary defined *mestizos (mestis)* as being children of a "European" and an "American" parent.

English usage is little different. John Wesley, in 1747, referred to First Nations, or Native American, people of Georgia as "the Americans." The Quaker traveler William Bartram, after a lengthy tour among the Creeks, Cherokees, and Choctaws in the 1770s, refers to them as "the Americans." Samuel Johnson's *Dictionary* (1827 edition) has "American [from America]. An aboriginal native of America; an inhabitant of America."

In 1875, Charles Maclaren in a British encyclopedia wrote of "the American race," "the color of the American," "the American natives," and "the Americans," by which he meant "the Americans of indigenous races." More recently (1986), the *Chronicle of Higher Education* noted that "Scientists Find Evidence of Earliest Americans" in northeastern Brazil, meaning that these "earliest Americans" were Native Americans.

Beginning in the 1740s through 1780s, British newspapers also began to refer to their British subjects on the Atlantic seaboard as Americans in the sense of Britons living in America. After the United States became independent in the 1780s, its new citizens began to refer to themselves as Americans, perhaps trying to identify with the famous and legendary Chief Tammany (known for being a friend to European settlers) and with the continent of America.

It is incorrect usage to refer to the United States simply as America. It is "of America," and America is the entire continent. California was part of America before it became part of the United States, and everything from Canada to Chile is still considered to be part of America. The concept of America as including more than just the United States is reflected in usage throughout the Americas. For example, in many parts of Latin America, U.S. citizens are referred to as "North Americans," with little effort made to distinguish between Canadians and U.S. Anglo-Americans. The Organization of American States is a group made up of representatives of nations throughout the Americas; it has nothing to do with the states of the United States. It is ironic that of all the nations in the Americas, the United States is the only one that has not come up with a term other than "Americans" to describe its citizens.

— J. Forbes

SEE ALSO:

American Indians; Tammany; Tammany Society.

AMERICAN FUR COMPANY

The American Fur Company was established by German immigrant John Jacob Astor in 1808. Fur trading was one of the earliest sources of profit for American businessmen, and by the early 1800s,

An early map of America, which includes as "North America" all of the known lands extending from Greenland into the area that borders South America (present-day Central America). The area of the present-day United States and Canada is marked by many unknown regions, including Alaska, the Pacific Northwest, and the Arctic. Also, California appears as an island cut off from the rest of the continent!

Astor had become a millionaire and the head of the most successful fur trading company in the United States.

Because the business was so competitive, traders were always looking for new sources of revenue; expanding west seemed profitable. From its origins at the mouth of the Columbia River, the American Fur Company stretched its operations through Minnesota, Iowa, and Kansas. Spreading along the Missouri River, fur companies also competed for trade in the territories of Nebraska, Colorado, and the Dakotas, and by the 1840s, non-Native American settlement in Oregon was underway.

As operations expanded, the traders' contact with American Indians also greatly increased. Businessmen like Astor recognized that their personal wealth depended upon maintaining favorable trading relations with the Native people of these regions. Businesses obtained their furs by bartering company goods for the pelts hunted by Native trappers. This system was so important that American Fur Company officials were known to replace gifts to tribal chiefs from rival companies with bigger and more expensive goods. Many American Indians took advantage of such rivalries to obtain better prices for their pelts. Fur company records also indicate that Native trappers often refused to trade goods that they did not consider worthy of their hunting efforts. Brass kettles, beads, and blankets were common trades. Beaver pelts could also gain the Native hunter access to weapons and gunpowder.

In 1834, John Astor retired. Eight years later, the company was taken over by Pierre Chateau and Company. By this time, the fur trade had significantly altered. The government's interest in acquiring developing regions led it to purchase the western land from the American fur traders. The fur companies profited from selling their interests and developed new sources of revenue from lumber and the railroads.

The land cession treaties signed by the American Indians were not nearly as favorable, however. When the Sioux, Ojibwe (Chippewa), and Winnebago tribes agreed to an 1837 treaty with the federal government, they gave up all of their land east of the Mississippi River. By opening their land to non-Indian settlement, they allowed the new occupants to share in what had previously been their own unique knowledge of the environment. Therefore, they quickly lost their influence over the fur trade. And without the financial backing enjoyed by the fur companies, these tribes did not have the opportunity to develop new trading relationships. Once their economic bargaining power was removed, these tribes were soon forced from the land they had previously ruled.

AMERICAN HORSE, THE ELDER
(d. 1877)

During the 1860s and 1870s, Washincun Tashunka, also known as American Horse or Iron Plume, was a leader of the Oglala Sioux and a prominent ally of his cousin Red Cloud, another major Sioux leader, in the fight over the Bozeman Trail. This fight was called Red Cloud's War, and its aim was to gain control of the passage between the present states of Wyoming and Montana. During the 1860s, Euro-American settlers and U.S. military personnel attempted to construct forts along the Bozeman Trail. Since the trail's discovery by John Bozeman in 1863, many settlers and miners had made their route through the passage illegally, as much of the trail went across land that was reserved by treaty for the Sioux and Cheyenne peoples.

Even with the signing of the Fort Laramie Treaty of 1868, in which the U.S. government seemingly awarded the Sioux and Cheyennes huge concessions on land and other issues, including protection by U.S. troops from incursions by settlers into Indian land, American Horse did not give up his objective for control of the Bozeman Trail. In 1870, American Horse accompanied Red Cloud to Washington, D.C., for a meeting with government officials that failed to bring assurances of peace and protection against settlers who were ignoring the treaty. In 1874, gold was discovered in the Black Hills of South Dakota, a land that was sacred to the Sioux. Miners and speculators swarmed to the Black Hills in greater numbers than ever and with no regard for the 1868 treaty that had made the area Sioux land. In 1876, American Horse once again took up arms in the fight for the Black Hills and in that year was also a part of the Battle of the Little Bighorn, during which George Armstrong

Custer and his Seventh Cavalry were defeated by Sioux and Cheyenne warriors.

The following September, a confrontation developed between U.S. soldiers and American Horse's band of Oglalas and Minniconjous. In the course of this confrontation, which was later to be known as the Battle of Slim Buttes, American Horse's group separated from Crazy Horse's band on the Grand River and started southward for the winter. A forward detachment from General George Crook's force, under the leadership of Captain Anson Mills, stumbled upon American Horse's encampment. The resulting attack on the camp was unsuccessful, but General Crook's force did manage to trap American Horse, four warriors, and fifteen women and children in a cave. General Crook soon arrived and directed the ensuing fighting, in which American Horse was wounded. Those who escaped alerted Sitting Bull and Gall, who rode with about six hundred warriors to help American Horse. Meanwhile, American Horse emerged from the cave, badly hurt from a bullet wound in his abdomen, and he died after refusing help from army surgeons.

American Horse's death and the destruction of his band's tipis and possessions were among a series of setbacks for the Sioux and their allies after their earlier victory at Little Bighorn. From 1877 through the present, the Sioux have been fighting—first on the battlefield and later in the courts—for the return of the Black Hills.

SEE ALSO:
Black Hills; Bozeman Trail and the Battle of a Hundred Slain; Crazy Horse; Crook, George; Custer, George Armstrong; Fort Laramie Treaty of 1868; Gall; Little Bighorn, Battle of the; Red Cloud; Sitting Bull.

American Horse (*right*) and Red Cloud, probably photographed sometime around 1870, when the two Sioux leaders (and cousins) attempted to convince the U.S. government to protect Native people from the influx of non-Indians who ignored Indians' treaty rights.

AMERICAN INDIAN ATHLETIC HALL OF FAME

Decades of athletic achievement by American Indians, primarily in football, basketball, baseball, and track, are enshrined in the American Indian Athletic Hall of Fame. The hall of fame is located on the campus of Haskell Indian Nations University in Lawrence, Kansas, and is incorporated under the state of Kansas.

The hall of fame, which pays tribute to American Indian athletes for their achievements, honors Olympic and professional greats such as Billy Mills, Jim Thorpe, Louis Tewanima, and Angelita Rosal. Stars from the 1920s up through the present are honored for their accomplishments. Each honoree has his or her picture and sports accomplishments engraved on a plaque on display for the public.

A twelve-person board of trustees selects the new honorees from nominations submitted to them. Candidates are chosen on the basis of playing ability, integrity, sportsmanship, character, and contributions to the team and to sports in general.

To be nominated as a potential honoree, an athlete must be a member of a tribe recognized by the federal government or have one-fourth degree of Indian blood. The athlete must have participated at a post–high school level in an amateur or professional sport recognized by the Amateur Athletic Union or the National Collegiate Athletic Association. The nominee must also have made a national impact in the sport.

People may submit names to the board of trustees. Those who do submit names must provide a nomination form, a photograph of the nominee, relevant newspaper clippings, and record book documentation.

The first fourteen athletes were inducted on November 25, 1972, at Kansas University with four hundred people in attendance. The keynote speaker was former U.S. Representative Ben Reifel, a Sioux from South Dakota.

Here is a list of names of the athletes enshrined in the American Indian Hall of Fame through the mid-1990s: Alexander Arcasa, Charles "Chief" Bender, Wilson "Buster" Charles, Albert A. Exendine, Joseph A. Guyon, Jimmie Johnson, John Levi, John "Chief" Meyers, Allie P. Reynolds, Theodore "Tiny" Roebuck, Reuben Sanders, Louis Tewanima, Jim Thorpe, Louis "Rabbit" Weller, Ellison Brown, Wallace Littlefinger, Elmer Busch, Albert Hawley, Frank Hudson, Frank Mt. Pleasant, Walter Johnson, Jesse "Cab" Renick, Gus Welch, Jimmine Wolf, Jr., Angelita Rosal, Bemus Pierce, Ed Rodgers, Louis R. Bruce (honorary), Robert L. Bennett (honorary), Chester (Chet) L. Ellis, Stacy S. Howell, Jack Jacobs, Clyde L. "Chief" James, Rollie Thurman Munsell, Phillip Osif, Frank W. "Mac" McDonald, Harold "Chuck"

Foster, Jr., William (Billy) Mervin Mills, Joseph "Bud" H. Sahmaunt, Joe Tindle Thornton, Egbert "Eg" Bryan Ward, Robert "Bob" Gawboy, Elijah "Eli" Smith, Martin Fredrick Wheelock, David W. Bray, Nelson B. Levering, Austin BenTincup, George P. Lovatta (honorary), Amos Aitson, George Levi, Thomas Cornelius Yarr, Turner A. Cochran (honorary), Sampson George Bird, Sidney M. Carney (honorary), Virgil R. Franklin, Robert E. Holmes, Gordon A. House, Peter "Pete" Hauser, Mayes McLain, Arthur S. Bensell, Alex "Sonny" Sixkiller, Wallace E. Galluzi (honorary), Clarence "Taffy" Abel, James Aron Ingram, Euel "Monk" Moore, Alvin LeRoy Williams, 1926 Haskell Indian Football Team, John "Johnny" Gene Allen, Edwin "Ed" Stanton Moore, Andrew "Andy" Hartley Payne, Jackson Sundown, Moses J. Yellowhorse, and Jack Claphan.

For further information, contact the American Indian Athletic Hall of Fame at the following address: Haskell Alumni Association, Haskell Indian Nations University, P.O. Box H-12, Lawrence, KS 66044.

SEE ALSO:
Baseball; Bender, Charles Albert; Haskell Indian Nations University; Mills, Billy; Reifel, Ben; Thorpe, Jim.

AMERICAN INDIAN CIVIL RIGHTS ACT OF 1968

In 1968, Congress passed the Indian Civil Rights Act, which repealed, or took back, Public Law 280. P.L. 280 had established as national policy the "termination" of Indian nations and tribes in their formal relationship with the government of the United States. It had also permitted states to assume civil and criminal jurisdiction over reservations. In contrast, the Civil Rights Act of 1968 required tribal consent for state action.

The Indian Civil Rights Act of 1968 actually became federal law as an amendment to another piece of civil rights legislation. The act provides for free speech, free exercise of religion, free press, peaceful assembly and petition, and other freedoms found under the first, fourth, fifth, sixth, eighth, and fourteenth amendments of the U.S. Constitution.

Despite the assurances of civil liberties provided by these amendments, the Indian Civil Rights Act has generated its share of controversy and dispute. Many Indian scholars and activists feel that, with the passage of the 1968 Civil Rights Act, Indian nations in effect fell victim to the U.S. Constitution's Bill of Rights, the very set of amendments intended to guarantee individual rights and liberties. These people point out that the emphasis on individual rights has led to the erosion of traditional customs in many Native communities. Many of the constitutional protections afforded by the act have also had the effect of reducing the absolute sovereign authority that Indian nations and tribes have traditionally exercised over their people. The law allows Indian nations to rely on traditional solutions only as long as they do not interfere with state and federal laws.

This has led many Indian activists to work for changes to the act in order to restore greater sovereignty and authority to tribal governments. Despite these problems, however, most tribal governments agreed that the act was an acceptable accommodation of tribal sovereignty with the status of individual Indians as U.S. citizens entitled to the civil liberties guaranteed by U.S. law. Also, in some areas, tribes have been exempted from compliance with the First Amendment's required separation of church and state, allowing Native spiritual beliefs and customs a greater role in tribal affairs.

In addition to issues involving religion, many other cases have arisen to either challenge or clarify the Indian Civil Rights Act. The first case to arise after the act was passed was that of *Dodge v. Nakai* in 1969. In that case, the Navajo Nation had excluded a non-Indian program director from its reservation. A federal judge struck down the tribal council's action as a violation of the director's civil rights.

Another case, a decade after the act was passed, involved the status of women in the tribe and the right of a tribe to determine its own membership. A woman who had married outside the tribe brought suit against the Santa Clara Pueblo because her children were not considered members of the tribe. Even so, male members of the tribe could marry outside the tribe and their children were considered members. The case was taken all the way to the U.S. Supreme Court. The decision was in favor of the tribal government.

Various issues regarding crime and punishment have also been raised by the Indian Civil Rights Act. For example, the act allows tribal courts to impose sentences on defendants only up to $500 in fines and/or six months in jail. More serious sentences, those handed down to people who have committed more serious crimes, are not covered by these provisions, and thus Indian nations and tribes have little power to deal with major criminal activity on their reservations. This places the judgment of major crimes on the shoulders of federal courts.

Congress did protect Indian religious freedom in the act by preventing tribal governments from making or enforcing laws prohibiting the free exercise of religion. However, this is a restriction on tribal governments only, not state governments. In states where P.L. 280 is in effect, if an Indian conducts ceremonies off the reservation, the 1968 act does not apply. In cases involving religious freedom, the states' interests outweigh the defendants' interests.

Critics of the act thus argue that despite its intention to guarantee Indian rights, the act has further confused both Indian nations and U.S. states as to which holds dominion over Native rights and responsibilities. Congress has allowed the use of compacts (agreements) between states and tribal governments in which they agree to share certain responsibilities. But the proposals are often confusing because of state laws that often override traditional law.

With larger numbers of Native people receiving degrees in law and other fields, both traditional law and laws such as the Indian Civil Rights Act of 1968 have been getting a close look from within Indian Country. Some Indian groups have been working on getting the act changed. Tribal judges are writing extensive opinion papers to accompany their judgments. These opinions are based on traditional law working together with the Bill of Rights and other federal and state laws.

— S. S. Davis

SEE ALSO:

Federal Recognition; General Allotment Act; House Concurrent Resolution 108; Indian Claims Commission Act; Meriam, Lewis; Relocation Program; Termination Policy; Wardship.

AMERICAN INDIAN CULTURE, CONTRIBUTIONS OF

SEE Native American Contributions.

AMERICAN INDIAN DANCE THEATRE

In 1987, the first professional theatrical troupe of Native American dancers began to tour the United States. The American Indian Dance Theatre was founded by New York producer Barbara Schwei in consultation with playwright Hanay Geiogamah, who has served as the company's director since its creation. Schwei and Geiogamah sought to share the beauty and artistry of Native American music and dance with the world. They recruited the top dancers and musicians from festivals, competitions, and powwows around the country in 1986 and launched their new dance company the following year in Colorado Springs, Colorado.

The American Indian Dance Theatre performs a variety of social dances from several tribes. They have received permission from various tribal councils to present traditional dances adapted for theatrical performance. Their repertoire is broad but not comprehensive: They do not perform dances from all tribes, and they do not perform sacred dances. The costumes of the dancers are spectacular and meaningful, such as the use of feathers in the Eagle Dance to represent power. The dancers themselves come from several different tribal backgrounds but work together as a single company.

In a few short years, the American Indian Dance Theatre has become internationally acclaimed, touring throughout the United States and the world. In both live and televised performances, it has captivated audiences with the energetic Fancy Dance, acrobatic Hoop Dance, and the delicate Butterfly Dance. As the dance company matures, it has struggled with such issues as how to honor the traditional form of the dance while presenting it theatrically, how to observe the division between sacred and social dance, and whether women's dancing is represented well enough in the program.

SEE ALSO:
Dance, American Indian; Feathers and Featherwork; Fancy Dance and Fancy Shawl Dance; Feathers and Featherwork; Festivals; Geiogamah, Hanay; Powwows; Regalia.

AMERICAN INDIAN EXPOSITION

The weeklong American Indian Exposition takes place each summer at the Caddo County Fairgrounds in Anadarko, Oklahoma. The exposition draws together Oklahoma's Southern Plains Indian tribes in a cultural celebration that includes song and dance competitions, arts and crafts exhibits and sales, a rodeo, a princess contest, parades, a carnival, a softball tournament, horse races, footraces, and many other events. One highlight is the "grand entry," a drum-centered circular parade that may include one hundred or more dancers of all ages in flamboyant regalia. For many Southern Plains Indians, the American Indian Exposition provides a chance to immerse themselves in various aspects of their cultural heritage, including feasting and camping in tipis. The American Indian Exposition is Indian owned and is operated by an independent board of directors, elected annually.

The first American Indian Exposition, then called the Southwest Indian Fair, was held jointly with the Caddo County Fair in September 1932. Early American Indian Exposition exhibits, displays, and events included canned and other prepared foods, livestock and poultry, miniature painted tipis, handmade dolls, bows and arrows, woven baskets, watercolor and oil paintings, pencil sketches, decorated tobacco pouches, rawhide saddle and riata (lasso) making, dog and horse travois (a frame slung between trailing pulls and pulled by a person or an animal), children's games, and flute and dance exhibitions.

The American Indian Exposition has always reflected the fact that Indian people of the southern Plains are invigorated by the musically rich activities of their tribes. Singers come to the exposition to present tribal songs of praise that they have composed. The drum is the heartbeat of many events, especially the intertribal dance competitions. For example, the war dance is a stately walk, with all dancers circling the drum, one step per beat. In gourd dancing (named after the gourd shakers that dancers carry), participants step in place to the beat of the drum and bend their knees when the drum tempo increases to a level called "honor beats." Round dancing is done in a side-by-side circle and involves stepping to a jagged rhythm. Other dance types include the men's straight dance and, recently influenced by the Northern Plains tribes, the women's jingle dress dance. During these dance competitions, the long, flowing fringes of the women's shawls and jingle dresses add excitement and color. Men wear long, rectangular, red and blue gourd dance shawls draped over their shoulders. All dances are characterized by a straight posture, a dignified manner, and a sincere effort to keep the dance in harmony with the beat of the drum—as some have said, to keep the dance always within the "voice of the drum."

A French airman stationed at nearby Sheppard Air Force Base leads off a ceremonial dance with a young Indian woman at the August 1951 American Indian Exposition in Anadarko, Oklahoma. Members of the armed forces of twelve Allied nations met Native Americans representing twenty-seven Indian nations at the event, which drew Indian people from the Southwest and Midwest.

SEE ALSO:
Dance, American Indian; Drums; Festivals; Powwows; Regalia; Tipi; War Dances.

AMERICAN INDIAN HIGHER EDUCATION CONSORTIUM

In 1972, tribal college leaders began the process of establishing the American Indian Higher Education Consortium (AIHEC) to promote unity and viable education options for Indians, especially those on reservations. Gerald One Feather of (then)

Oglala Sioux Community College; David Risling of D-Q (Deganawidah-Quetzalcoatl) University; Pat Locke, Hunkpapa Lakota, of the Western Interstate Commission for Higher Education; and Helen Schierbeck of the U.S. Office of Education organized the first meeting. Representatives from all seven tribal colleges and the three Bureau of Indian Affairs postsecondary institutions attended.

Mary Parker, a Seminole girl photographed at the Brighton Day School in 1941. Historically, education has been a complicated issue for Native people. Non-Native policy makers often saw education more as a way of getting Indians assimilated into the dominant culture than as a service that Indian people were capable of providing for themselves.

Five traits helped unify the colleges for their mutual benefit. They were all relatively isolated in the lowest income areas of the United States, and they all had small enrollments, Indian boards of regents, and a majority Native faculty and administration. "We had to take matters into our own hands and create institutions which would enrich our communities and give our young people a chance to grow and succeed," recalled Lionel Bordeaux, Sicangu Lakota, who became president of Sinte Gleska College in 1973, two years after its founding and was still president in 1994. He has also been president of AIHEC.

Historically, education has been a thorny issue for Native Americans. Treaty makers recognized its importance, almost always requiring educational services in return for ceded lands. Yet, when those treaty obligations were met—as they seldom were—the providers saw education only as a tool for assimilation, turning it into a destructive weapon. Seeing the value of education and also the role it had played historically, those founding leaders of AIHEC acknowledged the long-standing belief that only Native American people themselves could improve their lives and provide effective educa-

tion. Outside solutions imposed on tribal people for three hundred years not only failed the people but harmed tribal cultures. The most obvious strength of the colleges is that they are the only institutions able to deliver postsecondary services on the reservations. Now those colleges are at the forefront of the resurgence of Indian cultures and traditional values.

AIHEC incorporated as a nonprofit corporation in 1973 in Denver, Colorado, and selected its first full-time staff, with David M. Gipp, a Hunkpapa Lakota, as first executive director. The directors and staff decided to seek federal funding.

Like its tribal college members, AIHEC immediately made a conscious decision to stress Native culture, traditions, and spirituality. Sinte Gleska College's board chairman, Stanley Red Bird, Sicangu Lakota spiritual leader, offered special prayers for the consortium's members to solve the problems they faced.

Despite highly professional lobbying and education efforts led by Gipp and Bordeaux, AIHEC did not achieve establishing legislation for six years, until President Jimmy Carter signed the Tribally Controlled Community College Act of 1978. The

Bureau of Indian Affairs testified against the bill during congressional hearings. Most Congress members could not understand why legislation was necessary since the Navajo Community College (NCC) had obtained establishing legislation and federal funding in 1968. Senator James Abourezk, a Democrat from South Dakota, provided important leadership and support for the passage of the final bill after his election in 1975. Schierbeck, the only supportive federal official, provided invaluable support and funding assistance from the U.S. Office of Education.

NCC administrators and board had mixed feelings about the new organization but put aside concerns about increased competition for very limited funding in the interest of intertribal unity and the good of a united organization. Moving AIHEC headquarters to Washington, D.C., also created a bone of contention with some members who say it should remain in Indian Country. Also, while the colleges stress Indian leadership, by the early 1990s, most of AIHEC's staff was non-Indian.

Since 1978, AIHEC has grown from ten to twenty-seven member colleges with fourteen thousand full- and part-time students. Sinte Gleska at Rosebud is now a university, and both it and Pine Ridge Reservation's college, now Oglala Lakota College, offer accredited masters programs as well as associate and bachelor degrees. Salish Kootenai College in Pablo, Montana, also offers an accredited four-year program, and the others all have two-year associate degree programs.

Tribal colleges are chartered by their tribes and governed by Native American boards of trustees. Twelve of the colleges are fully accredited at the two-year level, and, in 1994, the others were in the process of achieving accreditation from their regional accrediting boards. Three BIA sponsored colleges—Haskell Indian Nations in Lawrence, Kansas; Southwest Indian Polytechnical Institute in Albuquerque, New Mexico; and the Institute of American Indian Arts in Santa Fe, New Mexico—are also part of the consortium.

Enrollment at the colleges, all in twelve midwestern and western states, ranges from one hundred to two thousand students. They are usually the only postsecondary institutions in rural areas to serve both Indian and non-Indian students. Over

Navajo Community College, in the Navajo Nation in Shiprock, Arizona, is one of dozens of tribal colleges that have contributed to the increase in Native student enrollments since the 1980s.

15 percent of tribal college students are non-Indians, but only Minnesota offers any state funding for its tribal college, Fond du Lac Community College.

During the 1980s, Native Americans were the only ethnic minority to increase their college enrollment, and most AIHEC students are the first in their families to attend college. The division of the small funding pie provides smaller and smaller portions to the colleges each year. Federal legislation entitles each full-time AIHEC student to $5,820 annually, but that funding level has never been reached. In 1989, at its lowest, funding was $1,964, and in 1993, it was authorized at $3,002 per student. Most reservations have no tax base to assist their colleges, nor do the colleges have a base of alumni to depend on yet.

Fund-raising through the American Indian College Fund, established as an independent entity in 1989, has become an important task for AIHEC. The fund set a goal of $10 million for its first five years and achieved $7 million in just over two years from foundations, grants, and individual contributors. "Lack of public awareness is the only thing that stands between the colleges and the funds they need, deserve, and can attract to operate at their fullest potential. People are eager to support this movement," said David Archambault, Lakota, president of the fund in 1991. That year, the fund launched its major media campaign with the theme "Save a culture that could save ours."

Only 10 percent of Indian reservation high school graduates have attended off-reservation colleges, and 90 percent of them dropped out or failed their first year. Yet a student who attends a tribal college for even one year is four times more likely to succeed at a mainstream college or university. More than 30 percent of tribal college graduates continue their higher education, and an estimated 80 percent of tribal college graduates are employed, most of them on reservations. Facilities range from new buildings constructed by students to old shopping centers, a remodeled fish-processing plant, and trailers. Oglala Lakota College calls itself the world's largest college campus with college centers in all nine districts on the 2,000,000-acre (810-hectare) reservation in addition to Rapid City, South Dakota.

In 1991, AIHEC's Telecommunications Proj-

A graduate of the Institute of American Indian Arts in Santa Fe, New Mexico, one of three colleges sponsored by the Bureau of Indian Affairs (BIA) that belongs to the American Indian Higher Education Consortium.

ect began installing both downlink and uplink satellite equipment to connect all the AIHEC colleges and provide a way for them to share instructors, classes, and other information. One example of its use is an Ojibwe student living on the Flathead Reservation in Montana studying her own language with an Ojibwe language instructor at Lac Courte Oreilles College in Wisconsin. AIHEC educators hope telecommunications courses can join all the institutions electronically.

AIHEC students' ages range from seventeen to seventy, and a majority are women in their thirties with families. Most of them could not hope to leave the reservation to get an education. Besides academic and vocational education, the colleges also offer general equivalency diplomas and literacy programs. AIHEC colleges also offer invaluable assistance to their tribes in research; development; sobriety and health services; leadership development; and retention of tribal cultures, histories, and customs.

The Carnegie Foundation for the Advancement of Teaching conducted a two-year study of tribally controlled colleges. Its 1989 report says the colleges "can be understood only in the historical context of Indian education and in the spiritual role they play in bringing renewal to their people."
— C. Hamilton

SEE ALSO:
Boarding Schools; D-Q University; Education, Indian; Institute of American Indian Arts; Navajo Community College.

AMERICAN INDIAN HISTORICAL SOCIETY

The American Indian Historical Society is an organization dedicated to historical research and teachings about Native Americans. It is involved in supporting Native issues throughout the United States. Its philosophy is that Native people can do what is necessary for their lives on the basis of their own strength, will, and volition. Accomplishments include assisting in the efforts of individual tribes to preserve their rights.

Located in San Francisco, California, the society was founded in 1964 by fifteen tribal Indians.

Indian people have always been at the helm of all the organization's activities and accomplishments. The main organizers were Rupert and Jeanette Henry Costo, and, from 1964 to 1989, Rupert Costo, a full-blood Cahuilla, served as the organization's president.

Beginning in 1964, the American Indian Historical Society published *The Indian Historian* for eighteen years. This journal featured articles on Native history from the Native viewpoint. Other publications of the society have included *Wassaja*, a national newspaper of Native America that was published from 1972 to 1984, and a popular publication for Indian children called *The Weewish Tree* (1974 to 1983).

The Indian Historian Press, a book publisher, is part of the society and is still in operation. *Textbooks and the American Indian*, its first book, was published in 1970. Over fifty books in all, some of them classics, have been published by the press to date. They include *Tsali*, by Denton Bedford; *Give or Take a Century: An Eskimo Saga*, by Joseph Senungetuk; *Indian Treaties*, by Rupert Costo; and the *Index to Literature on the American Indian*. The American Indian Historical Society no longer operates as a corporation, but it continues its work on a limited basis today.

SEE ALSO:
Costo, Rupert.

AMERICAN INDIAN MOVEMENT

AIM—the American Indian Movement—was founded in Minneapolis in 1968 by young urban Native activists including Clyde Bellecourt, Eddie Benton, Mary Jane Wilson, George Mitchell, and Dennis Banks. Most were Ojibwe (Chippewa) Natives from different reservations in Minnesota. They considered themselves twentieth-century warriors, intent upon stirring up the dust of the American landscape. AIM was thought to be similar to the Black Panthers, an African-American activist group begun in the 1960s, as their ideas and attitudes were often militant and controversial.

AIM grew out of the Red Power movement that had surfaced within the dramatic climate of

AIM leader Russell Means leads a group of activists gathered in 1993 to revive some of the issues that concerned AIM and other activist organizations during the takeover of Wounded Knee in 1973.

the 1960s civil rights movement. One of AIM's earliest activities was to monitor police patrols within Native neighborhoods in Minneapolis. There had been news of police harassment of and discrimination against Indian people; AIM sought to put an end to those alarming reports. Arrests of Native Americans and harassment quickly diminished under the watchful eye of the AIM patrols.

After AIM members organized themselves in Minneapolis, they expanded and created a chapter in Cleveland. It was there that they met Russell Means, who was to be a powerful influence in the group's future activities and who became the first board chairman of the Cleveland chapter. Means was an Oglala from the Pine Ridge Reservation and was instrumental in uniting Ojibwe and Sioux tribal members.

It was through the involvement of the Sioux that AIM found its spiritual platform and that the original members, many of whom were far removed from their tribal culture and religion, discovered their Native roots through newly enlisted spiritual leaders like Leonard Crow Dog and Wallace Black Elk. AIM also became known as a spiritual move-

ment since most of the members believe in the return to their traditional cultural ways. The four main principles that govern the movement are the pursuit of sovereignty, sobriety, self-determination, and spirituality.

The occupation of Alcatraz Island in California in 1969, led by a Native group called Indians of All Tribes, paved the way for future occupation protests of AIM. The Alcatraz event was not led or inspired by AIM, but among the occupants were several young people who later became prominent in AIM. The occupation lasted for over a year with the intention of reclaiming the island by Natives' "right of discovery," the same doctrine that Europeans used to claim parts of North America already inhabited by Native Americans. The occupation heralded the beginning of the Red Power movement and served as a spark to ignite the flames of protest that followed.

The movement became involved in the fishing rights struggle along with the Ojibwes. During this time, AIM endorsed the fundamental principle of tribal sovereignty, openly maintained arms, and adopted the United States flag flown upside down as its official symbol. The latter is an international distress signal for people in trouble. Clyde Bellecourt said that no one could deny that Indians were people in trouble and in need of assistance.

AIM began to expand its program to cities throughout the Midwest. John Trudell, who had participated in the 1969 occupation of Alcatraz Island, joined the movement. Vernon Bellecourt, Clyde's brother, and Joe Locust cofounded Denver (Colorado) AIM.

Beginning on July 4, 1971, AIM, along with other Indian rights groups such as the United Native Americans and United Indians of All Tribes, participated in a "countercelebration," an occupation at Mount Rushmore, the monument within the sacred Black Hills. The protest sought to restore the terms of the 1868 Treaty of Fort Laramie and return the Black Hills to the Lakota people; it also served to create a stronger sense of unity among Native Americans.

The following year, AIM took part in organizing a cross-country march on Washington, D.C.,

called the Trail of Broken Treaties. More than two thousand protesters convened on the eve of the 1972 presidential election at the Bureau of Indian Affairs (BIA) with a list of demands centering on Indian sovereignty issues. The federal officials refused to negotiate, and the activists took over the BIA building, barricading entry and rummaging through various documents within the building. After President Richard Nixon's administration promised to look into each issue raised in the protesters' negotiating paper, the protesters gave up their occupation after one week. But during the movement's time in the BIA, the members discovered files and documents that fueled their stance even more. Some of the documents that they discovered concerned the sterilization of young Indian women.

Soon after the BIA occupation, a protest in Custer, South Dakota, resulted in the burning of a courthouse. The protest was staged against the murder of an Indian, Wesley Bad Heart Bull, and the acquittal of his European-American killer.

A group photo of AIM leaders at a 1982 American Indian Movement conference in San Francisco. The conference drew prominent Indian activist leaders of the 1960s, 1970s, and 1980s.

A demonstration at Leavenworth Federal Penitentiary in support of AIM leader Leonard Peltier, convicted under suspicious circumstances of killing two FBI agents during a shootout at the Pine Ridge Reservation in 1975.

Many participants, including the victim's mother, were arrested, and the protests' outcome was unsuccessful; Bad Heart Bull's murderer never went to jail.

Also following the Trail of Broken Treaties protest came the occupation of Wounded Knee on the Oglala Pine Ridge Reservation in South Dakota. The siege at Wounded Knee began in 1973, when two hundred armed members of AIM, together with traditional Oglalas, opposed the tribal council of Pine Ridge. They charged Dick Wilson, the elected head of the federally sponsored tribal government, with corruption. The siege at Wounded Knee lasted for ten weeks and involved federal law enforcement officials, the BIA, local citizens, nationally prominent entertainment figures, and the national news media. The occupation resulted in the deaths of two Indians and one U.S. marshal paralyzed before it finally drew to an end. Occupiers were subject to arrest, and despite the lengthy protest, conditions on Pine Ridge worsened. The federal government brought criminal charges against Dennis Banks and Russell Means,

in an attempt to destroy the movement's leadership. Those charges were dismissed by a federal judge, who said, "The waters of justice had been polluted" by a government using the courts to promote a private agenda beyond the law.

On June 26, 1975, an AIM group that had been staying at the Jumping Bull Ranch on Pine Ridge Reservation was startled by FBI agents who had pursued a vehicle into the grounds of the ranch. What followed was a firefight that left one Native man and two agents dead. The group managed to escape the area, and the biggest manhunt in FBI history was conducted for the person or persons responsible for killing the agents.

Leonard Peltier, Robert Robideau, and Darrelle (Dino) Butler were indicted for the murder of the agents. Although they admitted firing upon the agents, Robideau and Butler were acquitted on grounds of self-defense since the judge took into account the climate of fear created by the government's ongoing tactics against AIM. Leonard Peltier was illegally extradited from Canada and tried separately. Although Peltier's trial was riddled with perjury and misinformation, as well as withheld evidence, he was convicted and is now serving two consecutive life sentences in Leavenworth Federal Penitentiary in Kansas.

John Trudell had served as a spokesperson for a national Leonard Peltier Defense Committee during the first of Peltier's appeals. On February 12, 1979, his house was firebombed; his wife, Tina Manning Trudell, their three children, and Tina's mother all died in the fire. Conjecture remains about the arsonists' goal: Was it to to stop Tina Trudell's work as an organizer to protect Duck Valley Reservation's water rights at Wildhorse Reservoir and put an end to her effective leadership on her reservation? Was it because John Trudell had spoken out strongly against the federal government—and burned an American flag—at the FBI building in Washington, D.C., the previous day? Both? In any case, John Trudell felt that having a national leadership for the American Indian Movement only provided a series of targets for the federal government to harass and prosecute. The national board was dissolved, but the movement continued to be organized on local levels.

There was at least one exception to the movement's march toward local autonomy. In 1974, Russell Means helped form the International Indian Treaty Council (IITC) to take a specific Native American issue to the United Nations. IITC, before the UN, charged the federal government with violating the 1868 Fort Laramie Treaty, an agreement by the federal government to abandon forts along the Bozeman Trail, a major settlers' passage to the West. Jimmie Durham, a Cherokee activist, expanded the IITC's agenda to include "issues of all indigenous nations" of the Western Hemisphere regarding their local and federal governments. IITC also organized a presentation of North, South, and Central Americans in front of the UN, prompting the formation of the UN's Working Group on Indigenous Populations. By the mid-1980s, however, the IITC had lost the backing of many traditional Natives and activists.

In 1978, AIM organized what was to be its last unified national action—The Longest Walk. The walk was meant to symbolize a history of Native Americans being forced to leave their homelands and the continuing problems Native Americans

AIM leader Leonard Peltier is photographed with his art in his prison cell in 1991. Peltier, who is serving two consecutive life sentences for shooting two FBI agents in South Dakota, is at the center of a drive to reinvestigate the circumstances surrounding the shootings, including the means by which evidence against him was acquired.

Members of the American Indian Movement and other demonstrators protest outside of the Metrodome in Minneapolis in January 1992. The object of their protest is the use of Indians as mascots by professional sports teams. The occasion for the protest is a football game between the Minnesota Vikings and the Washington Redskins. The Redskins are a team whose nickname is seen by many as an extreme form of the racism and disrespect for Indian cultures that pervades professional sports.

faced in their own country. By the time marchers had walked from San Francisco to Washington, D.C., doing community education along the way, they had gathered several hundred Natives from eighty nations to converge on the capital. There they reiterated the twenty-point program from the Trail of Broken Treaties march in 1972.

AIM's actions during the 1970s, though often filled with controversy and creating heated debate, did later prompt positive and beneficial reforms in BIA officers, policies, tribal leadership, and funding levels. The media attention to AIM stimulated Indian pride and unity and allowed the United States to become much more aware of and sensitive to Native American issues and concerns.

Local AIM actions continued during the 1980s. In South Dakota, the Black Hills Alliance has been successful in fighting uranium development. In 1981, the Dakota AIM established the Yellow Thunder Camp in the Black Hills and received legal recognition of the whole of the Black Hills, not just pieces of it, as a place of tremendous spiritual significance to the Lakotas, a place which they thus possessed special religious rights to. In

Arizona, AIM organized a security camp to protect more than ten thousand Navajos from forced relocation. In Colorado, AIM supported the Miskito Indians of Nicaragua during the mid-1980s and opposed the celebration of the Columbian Quincentennary in 1992. In Wisconsin, AIM helped Natives organize to protect their fishing rights established by treaty.

In 1994, there was a definite split in the movement. A group, some of whom were longtime AIM members, gathered in New Mexico and indicted Clyde Bellecourt, a cofounder of AIM, and his brother Vernon under several charges, including subversion of the American Indian Movement. The group, consisting of about seventeen AIM chapters, called itself the International Confederation of the Autonomous Chapters of the American Indian Movement and claimed autonomy from the Bellecourts' movement in Minneapolis. The confederation subpoenaed the Bellecourt brothers to attend a tribunal in which the brothers were found guilty of several of the charges. Many activists believed this would increase the gap within the movement and destroy the work.

Today, AIM membership has declined significantly. However, AIM is still pursuing the objectives of promoting Indian self-determination policies and recognition of treaty rights. Many of AIM's present-day activities include charitable, educational, and children's services programs for Native people; they emphasize ecological and environmental concerns.

But despite the apparent decline in AIM's role as a prime mover of Indian activism and political consciousness-raising, as Russell Means once said, "AIM never died. It only changed form. Anywhere Indians are standing up for themselves, whether they are struggling as individuals whose basic civil rights are being denied, as peoples whose human rights are being denied, as nations whose sovereign rights are being denied, or any combination of these factors, that's where you'll find the American Indian Movement. In that spirit of resistance to oppression, that's where you'll find AIM. In other words, AIM is now in every single Indian community, and it always will be."

— S. S. Davis / T. Midge / V. J. Weber

SEE ALSO:

Activism, Indian; Alcatraz Island, Occupation of; American Indian Resistance; Aquash, Anna Mae Pictou; Banks, Dennis; Bellecourt, Clyde and Vernon; Benton-Banai, Edward J.; Black Hills; Bozeman Trail and the Battle of a Hundred Slain; Bureau of Indian Affairs; Butler, Darrelle; Churchill, Ward; Crow Dog, Leonard; Fishing Rights; Fort Laramie Treaty of 1868; *Incident at Oglala*; Indian Activist Movement; Longest Walk; Means, Russell; Peltier, Leonard; Pine Ridge Reservation, Conflict at; Robideau, Robert; Self-determination; Trail of Broken Treaties; Treaties, Indian–United States; Tribal Sovereignty; Trudell, John; Trudell, Tina Manning; Wounded Knee, Confrontation at; Yellow Thunder Camp.

SUGGESTED READINGS:

Erdoes, Richard. *Crying for a Dream*. Santa Fe: Bear & Company Publishing, 1989.

F.B.I. Uniform Crime Reports. Washington, DC: Government Printing Office, 1975.

Hertzberg, Hazel W. "Indian Rights Movement, 1887–1973." *Handbook of North American Indians*: Vol. 1 of *History of Indian–White Relations*. Washington, DC: Smithsonian Institute, 1988.

Johansen, Bruce E. *Life and Death in Mohawk Country*. Golden, CO: North American Press/Fulcrum, 1993.

Johansen, Bruce E., and Roberto F. Maestas. *Wasi'chu: The Continuing Indian Wars*. New York: Monthly Review Press, 1979.

Matthiessen, Peter. *In the Spirit of Crazy Horse*. New York: Viking, 1983.

Nabokov, Peter. *Native American Testimony*. New York: Viking Penguin, 1991.

Weir, David, and Lowell Bergman, "The Killing of Anna Mae Aquash," *Rolling Stone*, April 7, 1977.

AMERICAN INDIAN POLICY REVIEW COMMISSION

Beginning in the mid-1960s, confrontations over treaty rights and federal Indian policy became commonplace across the United States. In the Northwest, "fish-ins" protesting restrictions on Native Americans' access to fishing provoked examination of century-old treaties. Alcatraz Island was occupied by Native American protesters in 1969, the Bureau of Indian Affairs in 1972, and Wounded Knee a year later. The American Indian Policy Review Commission (AIPRC) was convened by the federal government after that decade of unrest to examine the federal government's role in perpetuating poverty and injustice among Native Americans.

The commission, chaired by Senator James Abourezk, often worked with the United States Commission on Civil Rights. With task forces composed almost entirely of Native Americans, including some well-known activists of the 1970s, the AIPRC investigated social and economic conditions on reservations. It traveled around the United States from 1975 through 1977. In some respects, it found that little had changed since the compilation of the federal government's Meriam Report in the 1920s. Native Americans were still among the worst-paid and -housed people in the United States on the average, especially if they lived in rural areas. Health care was still falling short of needs. A 1977 AIPRC report found that the 1974 Self-determination Act had failed to bring true self-government to Indian reservations. The AIPRC has since investigated numerous issues regarding life in Native America, such as the growing use of Native nations as "energy colonies" as coal and uranium mining increased following the oil shortages of the 1970s.

SEE ALSO:
Alcatraz Island, Occupation of; American Indian Civil Rights Act of 1968; Bureau of Indian Affairs; Meriam, Lewis; Trail of Broken Treaties; Wounded Knee, Confrontation at (1973).

AMERICAN INDIAN PRESS ASSOCIATION

See Native American Journalists Association.

AMERICAN INDIAN RESISTANCE

Native Americans have been fighting the domination of European ways since the first decades of colonization. Usually, before 1890, wars of resistance were sparked as a Native nation's land base became too small to support its members in traditional fashion. In many of these wars of resistance, a particular Native American leader, such as Metacom (known as King Philip) or Tecumseh, rallied many Indian nations in a unified front. After subjugation of Native peoples by about 1900, resistance often went "underground" in the form of religious movements that were closed to non-Indians. With the reassertion of treaty rights late in the twentieth century, civil disobedience often was used as a tactic of resistance. The following examples provide illustrations of representative acts of Native resistance.

King Philip's War (1676)
In 1662, the mantle of leadership among the Wampanoags fell to Metacom, who was called King Philip by the English. Metacom distrusted nearly all Europeans and European-Americans. Throughout his childhood, Metacom had watched his people dwindle before the English advance. By 1671, about forty thousand people of European descent lived in New England. The Native population,

For decades, many Americans were exposed to this image of the 1890 Wounded Knee massacre as a "battle" pitting armed and mounted Indian warriors against U.S. troops. The reality behind the event, which took place largely as a military reaction to the Indians' act of quiet defiance against a U.S. ban on the Ghost Dance, was quite different, however, as hundreds of Indian men, women, and children were surrounded and killed by the soldiers.

Money Burns...
Land Is Forever.

SREE!

A contemporary expression of Native resistance to encroachment onto Indian land: a Pima woman and her sign protesting freeway construction at the Salt River Pima Reservation in Arizona.

double that of the Europeans before the Pequot War, was now about twenty thousand. European farms and pastures were crawling toward Mount Hope, driving away game, creating friction over land that the Indians had used without question for so many generations that they had lost count. By 1675, the Wampanoags held only a small strip of land at Mount Hope, and settlers wanted it.

Metacom grew more bitter by the day; he could see his nation being destroyed before his eyes. English cattle trampled Indian cornfields; farming forced game animals farther into the wilderness. He was summoned to Plymouth to answer questions, while other people in his nation were interrogated by Puritan officials. Traders fleeced Indians, exchanging furs for liquor. The devastation of alcohol and disease and the loss of land destroyed families and tradition. These were Metacom's thoughts as he prepared to go to war against the English.

By August 1676, the war ended, as the Mohawks and Mohegans opted out of their alliance with the Wampanoags, leaving after the English had exterminated the Narragansetts. Nearly all of Metacom's warriors, their families, and friends had been killed or driven into hiding. Metacom himself fled toward Mount Hope, then hid in a swamp. When English soldiers found him, they dragged him out of the mire and executed him.

In terms of deaths in proportion to total population, King Philip's War was among the deadliest in American history. About one thousand colonists died in the war; many more died of starvation and war-related diseases. Every Native nation bordering the Puritan settlements was reduced to ruin.

Pueblo Revolt (1680)

On the other side of the present-day United States, unable to wrest wealth from the land themselves, the colonists of New Mexico squeezed the Pueblos harshly for produce and labor. The priests railed against the Natives' "devil worship" and from time to time whipped some of the Pueblos' most respected elders (sometimes to death) in public displays. All of this fired resentment among the Native people. Fifty years after the first colonization, the Pueblos joined with their ancient enemies, the Apaches, in an effort to drive the Spanish out. This revolt failed.

Thirty years later, however, in 1680, a coalition of pueblos, unified by the war captain Popé, raised a furious revolt that killed a quarter of the settlers, trashed the hated churches, and sent the surviving Spanish down the trail to El Paso Norte, leaving behind almost everything they owned. The governor summed up the situation: "Today they [the Pueblos] are very happy without religio[n], or Spaniards."

Popé's policies after the rout of the Spanish proved too zealous for most Pueblos. He took on the airs of a petty tyrant and forbade his people to use anything that the Spanish had brought, including new crops. Most of Popé's edicts regarding crops were ignored. Popé even ordered the execution of some of his reputed enemies. The Pueblo confederacy that had expelled the Spanish then broke into two camps, one favoring Popé, the other opposing him. Popé was deposed but, in 1688, was restored shortly before he died. Four Spanish attempts at reconquest in eight years combined with a plague of European diseases and the existing civil war to depopulate the Pueblos' villages after Popé's death. In 1692, the Spanish returned to stay, until Mexican independence from Spain in 1821 made much of the current U.S. Southwest part of Mexico. In 1848, the United States in turn acquired this territory from Mexico.

Confederacies in the "Old Northwest" (1750–1820)

Significant pan-tribal efforts to slow down and stop the oncoming settlers in the Great Lakes area by Pontiac (Ottawa) in the eighteenth century and Tecumseh (Shawnee) in the early nineteenth century demonstrated the resolve of these peoples to resist European domination. At about 1800, a tide of humanity spilled across the mountains into the rich bottomlands of the Mississippi, the valley of the Ohio, northward, and westward. At the turn of the century, the non-Indian population of the Mississippi Valley was 377,000. By 1830, the non-Indian population of the same area had risen to 937,000.

Even before this migration of non-Indians, tribes after 1790 had tried to cooperate to head off this danger to their land and culture. Led by the Miami leader Little Turtle, a confederation that included elements of the Shawnees, Lenapes (Delawares), Wyandots, Miamis, and Ottawas told the United States in 1790 that settlers were not to travel beyond the Ohio River. Thousands of settlers were surging into the area, ignoring governmental edicts from both sides. In 1794, a force under the command of General "Mad Anthony" Wayne defeated the confederacy's warriors at Fallen Timbers. In 1795, most of present-day Ohio and parts of Indiana were surrendered at the Treaty of Greenville.

Native resistance surged again shortly after the turn of the century under the leadership of Tecumseh, or "Crouching Tiger" in his native Shawnee language. Tecumseh was born about 1768 near present-day Oldtown, Ohio, and fought with Turkey Foot at Fallen Timbers. Tecumseh's father, the Shawnee chief Pucksinwa, died at the Battle of Point Pleasant in 1774, at which time, Tecumseh (who was not quite ten) was said to have served with the British. Tecumseh's influence grew rapidly as he came of age after the American Revolution, not only because of his wisdom as a statesman and a warrior, but also because he forbade the torture of prisoners.

By the turn of the century, as the number of settlers grew, Tecumseh began to assemble the Shawnees, Lenapes, Ottawas, Ojibwes, Kickapoos, and Wyandots into a confederation. Their aim: to establish a permanent Native state to act as a buffer zone between the United States to the east and British Canada to the north. One European-American observer recalled Tecumseh as a commanding speaker. His voice was said to have "resounded over the multitude . . . his words like a succession of thunderbolts."

Territorial Governor William Henry Harrison tried to undermine the growing strength of Tecumseh's Native union by negotiating treaties of cession with individual tribes. Since only a portion of each tribe or nation's warriors elected to follow Tecumseh, Harrison found it easy enough to find "treaty Indians" among those who did not elect to fight. By 1811, Harrison negotiated at least fifteen treaties, all of which Tecumseh rejected as invalid.

Tecumseh was particularly galled by Harrison's treaty of September 30, 1809, with the Lenapes, Potawatomies, Miamis, Kickapoos, and Eel River peoples. For $8,200 in cash and $2,350 in annuities, Harrison had laid claim for the United States to some 3 million acres (1.2 million hectares) of rich hunting land along the Wabash River in the

A woman wearing a button proclaiming "Aboriginal Solidarity" joins other activists from throughout North America demonstrating their support for Native rights and sovereignty in Oka, Quebec.

heart of the area where Tecumseh wished to erect his Indian nation.

During 1811, bands of warriors in league with Tecumseh began ranging out of the settlement of Tippecanoe to terrorize nearby farmsteads and small backwoods settlements. Harrison said he would wipe out Tippecanoe if the raids did not stop; Tecumseh said they would stop when the land signed away under the 1810 treaty was returned. Tecumseh then journeyed southward to bring the Creeks, Chickasaws, and Choctaws into his alliance. While he was traveling, the command of the existing alliance fell to Tecumseh's brother, who was called the Prophet.

On September 26, 1811, Harrison departed Vincennes, in present-day Indiana, with more than nine hundred men, two-thirds of them Native allies. Within two hours of pitched battle, Harrison's forces routed the Natives, then burned the village of Tippecanoe as Tecumseh's forces scattered into the woods. Having committed twenty thousand men and $5 million to the cause, the United States had effectively terminated armed Native resistance in the Ohio Valley and surrounding areas. (Harrison would later popularize this battle with Tecumseh at Tippecanoe in his successful campaign for the presidency with the campaign slogan "Tippecanoe and Tyler Too." John Tyler was Harrison's candidate for vice president.)

Returning from his travels to find his people defeated by Harrison's forces, Tecumseh fled to British Canada. During the War of 1812, he was put in command of a force of European-Americans and Natives as a British brigadier general. Harrison's forces met Tecumseh again at the Battle of the Thames. Tecumseh was killed during that battle.

Religious Resistance

As the last remnants of independent Native nations were subjugated in the last half of the nineteenth century, resistance often went "underground," often in the form of new religious movements. Religion was not a new form of resistance in Indian Country, however. From the days of the Delaware Prophet and Handsome Lake (who founded their religious movements in response to eighteenth-

A banner written in French and English proclaims the unfriendly welcome awaiting this Canadian army armored vehicle in Quebec. In recent decades, Mohawk communities on both sides of the U.S.–Canadian border have been embroiled in many issues affecting tribal leadership and economics. Reserves on the Canadian side have been particularly affected by confrontation and violence.

from Oregon to Nebraska into the Dakotas, where Sitting Bull endorsed its vision of a restoration of Native power and culture.

Wovoka's English name was Jack Wilson. Born a Paiute, he had spent his childhood after age fourteen with a Euro-American Christian family. Wovoka's father regularly read the Bible at meals. As Handsome Lake did before him, Wovoka combined Native and Christian symbols into a religion that evoked a messiah not in a person but in the promised delivery of Native people from the misery that came with subjugation by Euro-Americans. Wovoka's instructions to Ghost Dancers contained references to Christ as well as prophecies of Native restoration: "Do not tell the white people about this. Jesus is now upon the earth. He appears like a cloud. The dead are all alive again. I do not know when they will be here; maybe this fall or in the spring. When the time comes there will be no more sickness and everyone will be young again."

The Sioux took to the Ghost Dance with a frenzy that Wovoka had not anticipated, Sioux medicine men also said that special Ghost Shirts would shield the Sioux from soldiers' bullets. Driven by hunger, desperation, and a determined desire to escape from their new brutal reality, many Sioux ghost dancers worked themselves into a frenzy, during which they said they had seen the return of the buffalo and spoken with dead relatives.

By late 1890, an estimated thirty-five hundred Natives were gathered near Wounded Knee Creek, which bisects the Pine Ridge Indian Reservation. Many of them demanded the right to practice the Ghost Dance religion, which held that God would create new worlds for them in which the buffalo would return and white men would vanish. The rules of the reservation laid down by the Indian Bureau forbade practice of the religion. Perfor-

century subjugation in the East), religious movements had become a powerful force in resisting the Euro-American invasion.

By 1890, the remaining Lakotas were corralled into concentration camp conditions on the Plains. The Ghost Dance religion arrived when the people's spirits were at their lowest ebb. Spawned by the prophet Wovoka, a Paiute, the Ghost Dance spread among the destitute Native peoples of the West,

mance of the dance helped to spark the massacre at Wounded Knee, where the U.S. Seventh Cavalry gunned down and fatally beat 146 Native men, women, and children.

Wovoka was deeply saddened by the massacre. The bloody result convinced Wovoka that the religion ought to be abandoned. Sadly, Wovoka told his followers that the path he had advised them to follow was now choked with sand and covered with grass. "My children," he preached, "I call upon you to travel a new trail, the only trail now open—the White Man's Road."

Twentieth-Century Resistance

Early in the twentieth century, religion continued to be one of the most formidable vehicles of Native American resistance to domination. The Native American Church was founded in 1918 and continued to attract American Indians throughout the twentieth century. Older Native religions, such as the Code of Handsome Lake among the Iroquois, are still widely and actively practiced at the turn of the twentieth century into the twenty-first century.

During the last half of the twentieth century, civil disobedience was used more often (often in tandem with legal actions) to defend treaty rights. Modern civil disobedience began with "fish-ins" in the Pacific Northwest during the 1960s. Native people in Puget Sound challenged state limitations on their treaty-guaranteed rights to fish.

The American Indian Movement (AIM) was formed in 1968, with civil disobedience as its primary focus. The organization allied with others to occupy Alcatraz Island in 1969 and to seize the Bureau of Indian Affairs headquarters in November 1972. A year later, AIM occupied the hamlet of Wounded Knee to dramatize the abrogation of treaty rights nationwide. In a similar manner, Mohawks at Oka, Quebec, in 1990 endured a months-long standoff with police and the Canadian army over land rights.

With the decline of AIM's influence as a lightning rod for Indian activism and resistance has come a new type of resistance to the lot of Indians at the hands of the dominant North American culture. Activist organizations such as AIM have turned their energies to improving the health, food, and social services available to Native people, particularly those living on reservations, and Indians con-

tinue to fight against treaty abuses and violations, primarily through the courts.

— B. E. Johansen

SEE ALSO:

Activism, Indian; Alcatraz Island, Occupation of; American Indian Movement; Fallen Timbers, Battle of; Fishing Rights; Ghost Dance Religion; Handsome Lake; Indian Activist Movement; Kahnawake Mohawks; King Philip's War; Longhouse Religion; Mohawk; Mohawk Warrior Society; Narragansett; Native American Church; Pan-Indian (Intertribal) Movements; Pequot War; Pontiac; Pontiac's War; Pueblo Revolt of 1680; Tecumseh; Treaties, Indian–United States; Tribal Sovereignty; Wampanoag; Wounded Knee (1890); Wounded Knee, Confrontation at (1973); Wovoka; Yellow Thunder Camp.

SUGGESTED READINGS:

Johansen, Bruce E. *Life and Death in Mohawk Country.* Golden, CO: North American Press/Fulcrum, 1993.

McNickle, D'Arcy. *They Came Here First: The Epic of the American Indian.* New York: Harper & Row Perennial Library, 1975.

Slotkin, Richard, and James K. Folsom, eds. *So Dreadful a Judgment: Puritan Responses to King Philip's War 1676–1677.* Middleton, CT: Wesleyan University Press, 1978.

Tebbel, John, and Keith Jennison. *The American Indian Wars.* New York: Bonanza Books, 1960.

AMERICAN INDIANS

In the years before 1492, Europeans used the word *India* to refer to a vast region beyond (to the east of) Persia (present-day Iran) and the Arabian Peninsula (present-day Saudi Arabia and several smaller states). *India*, as a term, was derived from Indus, the name of a very large river that flows through today's Pakistan.

The Greeks and Romans knew of India, and the name was also spread widely by Persians and Arabs, sometimes with an *h* in front of it, as in Hindustan (the kingdom of India, or India-stan). The people of India were called *indos* in Latin, which became *indios* in Spanish, *indiani* in Italian, *indienne* in French, *Ind* or *Hind* in the English of William

A vendor at a market in Ecuador. Like other Native people throughout the Americas, this woman is descended from one of the many indigenous peoples whom the Spanish colonizers referred to as *indios,* or "Indians."

years earlier, he had personally met a man and a woman who had reached Galway, Ireland, coming from the west. He believed they were from Catayo but they were probably from America (which in its purest sense refers to all of North, South, and Central America, the Caribbean, and Greenland).

When Columbus met people in the Caribbean region, he immediately began referring to them as *indios* in Spanish and *indos* in his letters in Latin. Other Spaniards soon followed his example, and soon all of the peoples visited by Europeans in North America, the Caribbean, South America, the Pacific, the Philippines, Indonesia, and the Far East were all called "Indians." Thus, we find the Spaniards speaking of Chinese Indians, Japanese Indians, Filipino Indians, and Indians of the Indies. America (that is, all of the "Americas") came to be known in Spanish circles as *las Indias* or "the Indies" and especially as "the West Indies" in contrast to "the East Indies" (Indonesia, Indochina, and India).

For many years, European writers mistakenly referred to the Native Americans as Indians, failing to realize how distant America is from the real India. In recent times, the term *American Indian* was coined to make it clear that the First Americans were not Indians of India. In Britain, the term *Red Indians* has been used to differentiate North American Natives from the "Brown Indians" of India.

At first, all Native people of America were referred to as Indians, but anthropologists began to make a distinction between peoples speaking Inuit (Eskimo) languages and peoples speaking Algonquian, Athabascan, and other languages. The Inuit were to be called Eskimos, while the others were to be known as Indians. This was done in spite of

Shakespeare's day, or the sixteenth and seventeenth century.

Many Europeans believed that one could sail directly west from Spain and reach Asia. East Asia at the time was thought of as India proper. *India extra gangem,* meaning "India east of the Ganges River," included what we now know as Indonesia, Indochina, China, Japan, and all offshore islands. Thus, when Columbus sailed west in 1492, he was sure that he would reach Catayo (China), Zipangu (Japan), and other parts of India. Indeed, a few

A mixing of American cultures, one from the Northeast and the other from the Southeast United States: The Narragansett ancestors of this woman, a participant in a traditional clothing contest at the Santa Fe Indian market in New Mexico, once thrived in present-day New England.

the fact that neither group's members were really Indians (neither being from India) and that many Inuit-speaking people cannot be physically distinguished from their Athabascan, Algonquian, or other neighbors.

The term *American Indian* was shortened to *Amerindian* in the twentieth century by some non-Native writers. This word has been especially used by British anthropologists writing about the indigenous people of the areas of Trinidad, Guyana, and Surinam, where many true Indians from India were brought in as agricultural workers in the nineteenth century. Thus, to avoid confusion between Indians from India and American Indians, the latter was shortened to Amerindian. A very small number of white writers have shortened it still further to *Amerind* (which is like calling European-Americans *Eurams* and African-Americans *Afroams* or *Aframs*.)

In recent years, large numbers of true Indians from India have been migrating to Canada and the United States. Many of these Indians now have children born in North America. These young people, like the Indians of Jamaica, Trinidad, and Guyana are now also "Americans." In the United States, they are calling themselves Indians, Indo-Americans, and Indian-Americans. In some instances, North Americans of Indian or Pakistani extraction are referred to as East Indian-Americans, although no doubt many Pakistanis would prefer not to be mistaken for East Indians, as they are indeed from a nation with an identity and political and religious outlooks that are in many ways different from those of India.

Despite the misnomers and possible confusion of identities, many Native people—including many Native writers and editors—feel comfortable describing themselves as Indians or American Indians since these are terms that they have long used to describe themselves, and they consider their historical and contemporary identity as American Indians to be unique and culturally rich. But other Native Americans feel that, along with Amerindian (which is rarely used these days by Native people), the term *American Indian* is less useful since Native Americans are not really Indians, and confusion often results when "America" and "Indian" are combined. For this reason, some indigenous Americans (Original Americans) are using other names for themselves such as aboriginal, First American, indigenous people, Native People, Native Americans, First Nations People, and Abya Yala People (from a Cuna name for America).

— J. D. Forbes

SEE ALSO:
America and *Americans*; India; Native American.

AMERICAN INDIAN SCIENCE AND ENGINEERING SOCIETY

In 1977, Andy Anderson, a Mohawk and Union Carbide engineer, convened a meeting of American Indian scientists and engineers in Wind Rock, Arizona, and established the American Indian Science and Engineering Society (AISES). This organization recruits and encourages Indians to enter engineering and science-related careers and helps develop technologically informed leaders within the Indian community. Founding members were Anderson; Jerry Elliott, Osage-Cherokee; Carol Metcalf Gardipe, Penobscot; Al Qoyawayma, Hopi; Jim Shorty, Navajo; and George Thomas, Cherokee.

In 1988, AISES, based in Boulder, Colorado, had just under 1,000 members and provided $1,400 in scholarships to Indian students in various sciences including engineering. By 1994, scholarship funds had reached more than $505,000 for 650 students, and membership had reached 2,700 with 100 college chapters. Lifetime members, known as the Sequoyah Fellowship, who make personal contributions of $1,000 or more, grew by 54 percent in 1993. Members include professionals, students, affiliate schools from kindergarten through twelfth grade, and college chapters.

AISES award winners in 1993 included a Navajo medical doctor, a Navajo-San Juan-Taos Pueblo civil and environmental engineering student, an elementary teacher at Turtle Mountain Elementary School, a Choctaw industrial engineering student, a Piscataway physics-electrical engineering student, a Choctaw math education major; and the Stanford University AISES Chapter.

AISES assists students and teachers from kindergarten through college graduate programs and works with both Indian and non-Indian people and orga-

An information booth on careers related to science and engineering at a 1995 conference of the American Indian Science and Engineering Society.

nizations to protect and improve the environment and increase scientific, medical, and engineering skills, interests, and curricula. The AISES Clearinghouse reviews materials prepared specifically for Indian students from kindergarten through the twelfth grade.

"American Indian history tells us that our ancestors were great scientists. We must continue today—practicing our culture and making a place for ourselves in today's world," said Carol Manning Nichols, Seneca Sequoyah Fellow and a scientist with Eastman Kodak.

The American Indian Knowledge Series, conceived and cosponsored by author-educator Vine Deloria, Jr., a Hunkpapa Lakota, brings together elders and lore keepers from various tribes to present and discuss their knowledge and traditions about the natural world. The sessions are presented by Indians to Indians with the information handled in a culturally and spiritually respectful manner.

The Environmental Institute, dedicated in October 1993 in Grants, Colorado, provides a facility for

camps, training sessions, and workshops. It includes a ten-station state-of-the-art IBM-donated computer laboratory. In 1993, the AISES Fair drew almost 500 Indian students from thirteen states. Another 170 middle and high school students from fifty-four tribes and twenty-one states attended the 1993 AISES Comprehensive Enrichment Programs at eight colleges. Nineteen teachers attended the Humans in the Environment workshop, an annual event preceding the AISES annual conference. AISES teachers also meet throughout the year to plan and develop projects.

AISES Leadership Conferences help college chapters with leadership skills and stresses Native traditions and professional goals. A mentoring program connects high school students interested in the various science areas with AISES college students. Eighty percent of AISES students complete college. *Pathways* is a publication that serves both students and professionals by providing lists of job openings and Indian science professionals.

The society's Science of Alcohol Curriculum

for American Indians for grades four through nine combines science, tribal cultures, and abuse prevention through stories, hands-on activities, and cooperative learning. AISES has also developed a Theatre Project to increase understanding of American Indian history and awareness of the environmental emergency facing American society in general. *Winds of Change*, the organization's award-winning quarterly magazine with a readership of one hundred thousand, provides an income for the organization, and 80 percent of its readership make it a permanent part of their library.

"The American Indian Science and Engineering Society is a gift from the Creator," said Norbert S. Hill, Oneida, AISES executive director in 1994. "As an Indian organization, we dance between the finest hopes and the greatest fears. We attempt to stay centered as we try to bring reality to our dreams of the past, the present, and the future. AISES will help write the history of our future."

— C. Hamilton

SEE ALSO:
Deloria, Vine, Jr.

AMERICAN REVOLUTION

Native American involvement was crucial to the course of the American War of Independence, which is more popularly known simply as the American Revolution. Native alliances, especially with the powerful Haudenosaunee (Iroquois or Six Nations) Confederacy, helped shape the outcome of the war. The war was also crucial for the Iroquois Confederacy, which split its alliance for the first time in several hundred years of its history. The Oneidas allied with the American revolutionaries and assisted George Washington's army during its most difficult winter. On the other hand, most of the Mohawks and Senecas sided with the British and suffered from brutal raids by the colonists, principally by troops under the command of General John Sullivan.

The effect of Native Americans on the course of the American Revolution may be surveyed through the lives of a half dozen Native people. Most were Iroquois because the People of the Long-

house occupied a strategic position in the military tactics (and geography) of the Revolution.

Son of a Black father and a Massachusett Indian mother, Crispus Attucks (c. 1725–1770) was the first casualty of the Boston Massacre of March 5, 1770, the first death in the cause of the American Revolution. During the Boston Massacre, which occurred five years before the first sustained combat of the American Revolution, Boston residents who were upset with the Townsend Acts (which directed them to pay unwanted taxes) attacked a detachment of British troops in front of the city's Customs House. The troops fired into the rioters, killing Attucks first. Some accounts say that Attucks was their leader. Two others died on the spot of gunshot wounds, and two more died of their injuries later. In 1888, a monument to Attucks was erected on the Boston Common.

The Seneca leader Cornplanter was a major Iroquois leader during the American Revolution; he figured importantly in the shifting alliances that accompanied the American Revolution and later became a personal friend of George Washington. Cornplanter generally favored neutrality in the American Revolution, but the Iroquois Grand Council could not reach consensus on alliance. On the other hand, Mohawk leader Joseph Brant (Thayendanegea) spoke eloquently about the necessity of taking up the hatchet, stating that neutrality would lead to disaster and that the Americans or the British might turn on the confederacy with a vengeance. Red Jacket and Cornplanter argued against Brant. They insisted that this quarrel was among the Euro-Americans; interfering in something they did not fully understand was a mistake. As the meeting broke up in a furor, Brant called Cornplanter a coward.

The people gathered at the grand council divided into two camps and discussed the issue of going to war. While most of the Senecas were disposed to neutrality, the words of Brant stung their ears; they could not bear to be called cowards. Finally, after lengthy discussion, the Senecas were swayed along with other wavering groups to take up the king's cause. The clan mothers consented also. The Senecas took this defeat gracefully and exhorted the warriors to unite in the fight against the Americans. With this meeting, the resolution was made unanimous. Thus did the majority of the Six

Nations break its neutrality and take up the British cause.

In the years prior to the War of Independence, Joseph Brant had been the personal secretary to British Indian Agent Sir William Johnson and had recruited a sizable number of Iroquois to the British interest until Johnson's death in 1774. After Johnson's death, Brant became secretary to his nephew Guy Johnson, who had taken over the Indian superintendency for the crown. As a Mohawk leader, Brant attended meetings of the Iroquois Grand Council at Onondaga and provided firsthand intelligence to the British military.

Drawing upon his influence among the Iroquois and his close diplomatic relationship with England, Brant played a major role in rallying the majority of the Iroquois to the British cause. Brant had been told that some Mohawk lands would be returned to them if they allied with the British. It was after returning to North America from Britain that Brant recruited most of the Mohawks, Senecas, Cayugas, and Onondagas to support the British. With the success of his efforts among these nations and his failure to dissuade most of the Oneidas and Tuscaroras from supporting the revolutionaries, the League of the Iroquois was split for the first time in several hundred years.

Brant's ferocity as a warrior was legendary; many settlers who supported the Americans called him "Monster Brant." The revolutionaries were no less fierce; revolutionary forces often adopted a scorched-earth policy against Iroquois who supported the British. George Washington's forces ended the battle for the Mohawk Valley by defeating the British and their Iroquois allies at the battle of Johnstown.

An undated color engraving by Howard Pyle of the March 5, 1770, Boston Massacre. Crispus Attucks, of mixed African and Massachusett Indian stock, lies slain, the first American casualty in service to the conflict that would become known as the American Revolution.

Brant's sister Mohawk Mary (or Molly) Brant (c. 1735–c. 1795) married Sir William Johnson and also wielded considerable influence on both sides of the frontier. She brought many Iroquois to the side of the British in the American Revolution. Because of her position, Mary was actually more influential within the Iroquois Confederacy than her younger brother, Joseph. As a clan mother and consort of Sir William, she was a powerful figure within the traditional framework. She also knew the ways of the white man. An observer commented that "one word from her goes further with them than a thousand from any white Man."

The Oneida Skenandoah (c. 1710–1816), who lived at Oneida Castle, New York, supported the British in the French and Indian War (1754–1763) but switched his allegiance to the revolutionaries in the American Revolution. Although Skenandoah asserted the Oneidas' official neutrality at the beginning of the Revolution, he supplied warriors and intelligence to the patriots, along with the Tuscaroras. As Washington's army shivered in the snow at Valley Forge, Skenandoah's Oneidas carried three hundred bushels of corn to the starving troops. Washington later named the Shenandoah Valley after the Oneida chief in appreciation of his support. During September of 1778, Skenandoah also supplied a key warning to residents of German Flats, near Albany, that their settlements were about to be raided by the British with their Iroquois allies under Joseph Brant. The settlers were thus able to get out of the area in time, but their homes and farms were burned and their livestock captured.

The Seneca Red Jacket (c. 1760–1830), a nephew of Handsome Lake, was probably best known as an ally of the British in the American Revolution. The name *Red Jacket* came from a scarlet coat given to him by the British for fighting with them during the Revolution.

The war ended along the American frontier, but the efforts of the Iroquois went unrewarded by both sides. The British discarded their Mohawk, Onondaga, Cayuga, and Seneca allies at their earliest convenience. The Americans did the same to their own allies, the Tuscaroras and Oneidas. At the conclusion of the Revolutionary War, the border between the new United States and Canada (still under British dominion) was drawn straight through the middle of Iroquois Country, without consultation.

In many respects, the legacy of Iroquois involvement in the war is evident today. Many Iroquois communities presently in Canada, such as the Six Nations Reserve in Brantford, Ontario, drew their numbers from Indians fleeing the United States after the Revolution. One of the best-known Indian reservations, the Akwesasne, or St. Regis, Mohawk Reservation is split among New York State on the United States side of the U.S.–Canadian border and the provinces of Quebec and Ontario on the Canadian side. Akwesasne has at times resembled a jigsaw puzzle politically, geographical-

ly, and culturally, with various factions at times rising up against one another and the Canadian military over such issues as tribal leadership, gaming, and commerce.

—B. E. Johansen

SEE ALSO:

Attucks, Crispus; Brant, Joseph; Cornplanter; Handsome Lake; Iroquois Confederacy; Johnson, Sir William; Red Jacket; Revere, Paul; Skenandoah; Washington, George.

SUGGESTED READINGS:

Armstrong, Virginia Irving, comp. *I Have Spoken: American History Through the Voices of the Indians*. Chicago: Swallow Books, 1971.

Edmunds, R. David. *American Indian Leaders: Studies in Diversity*. Lincoln: University of Nebraska Press, 1980.

Graymont, Barbara. *The Iroquois in the American Revolution*. Syracuse: Syracuse University Press, 1972.

Grinde, Donald A., Jr. *The Iroquois and the Founding of the American Nation*. San Francisco: Indian Historian Press, 1977.

Kelsay, Isabel Thompson. *Joseph Brant*. Syracuse: Syracuse University Press, 1984.

Stone, William L. *The Life and Times of Say-go-ye-wat-ha, or Red Jacket*. Albany, NY: Munsell, 1866.

Waters, Frank. *Brave Are My People*. Santa Fe: Clear Light, 1992.

AMERINDIANS

See *America* and *Americans*; American Indians; Native American.

ANASAZI

Anasazi is a Navajo word that was adopted by archaeologist A. V. Kidder to apply to a stage of Pueblo Indian culture that flourished in the Four Corners region of the Southwest before the arrival of Europeans. The Four Corners region is the area where Colorado, New Mexico, Arizona, and Utah meet. The Navajo term from which the name *Anasazi* derives has been variously translated into

A tower stands out among ancient Anasazi ruins at sunset at Cedar Mesa, Utah, in the Four Corners region where Utah, Colorado, New Mexico, and Arizona meet at a single point. Anasazi civilization laid the groundwork for other cultures in the area before disappearing several hundred years ago.

English, but the most common meaning now associated with the name is "Ancient Ones."

Archaeology is a young science; the first diggings in Europe date only to the nineteenth century. Thus, it is not surprising that when non-Indians first entered the Southwest and tried to account for the ruins within the region, they did not immediately realize that they had been built and abandoned by ancestors of the Pueblo Indians. There was wild speculation about their origin and antiquity. By the end of the first quarter of the twentieth century, however, archaeology had made significant strides, among them the discovery of the tree-ring dating method (dendrochronology) and other advances that helped to place the ruins within a historical perspective.

By 1927, the leading archaeologists of the Southwest gathered for what has come to be known as the First Pecos Conference. At this time, the Anasazis, rather than being viewed as a vanished race, as had been previously thought, were known to occupy a place in the cultural evolution of the Pueblo people. This conference divided that cultural evolution into nine stages, with three of them designated as Basketmaker and six of them designated as Pueblo. They are Basketmaker I, II, and III, and Pueblo I, II, III, IV, V, and VI, with Pueblo VI representing the contemporary Pueblo people of the Southwest. The periods most closely associated with Anasazi ruins are Pueblo II and Pueblo III.

The stages of Basketmaker I, II, and III trace the evolution of Archaic Desert Culture people from at least as early as 4000 B.C.E., from a nomadic hunting and gathering culture to a people with an increased dependence upon agriculture. At the same time, these people developed a rudimentary pottery, adopted the bow and arrow, and constructed pit houses for shelter, all of which had occurred by about 700 C.E.

Pueblo I is a transition phase, from about 700 C.E. to about 900 C.E., a period of dynamic change. Dwellings began being built entirely above ground, as rectangular single-story structures, while pit houses were converted into kivas (underground chambers) for ceremonial use. Pottery became increasingly more important.

The Pueblo II period, from 900 C.E. to 1100 C.E., saw the emergence of classic Anasazi architectural arrangements—rectangular multistory stone masonry apartments with adjacent rooms, fronted on the south by a kiva and a trash dump. The kiva is at the heart of Anasazi Culture, but it is the trash dump that is dear to the hearts of archaeologists. Much of what is known about the Anasazis comes from the study of their discarded items. During the Pueblo II period, pottery was improved by being made with thin coils of tempered clay, and cotton was introduced via trade routes with Mexico. This period also saw the spectacular development of Chaco Canyon as a regional economic center.

The Pueblo III period, 1100 C.E. to 1300 C.E., known as the classic Anasazi era, saw both the height of Anasazi Culture and its collapse. Anasazi settlements had grown to be large population centers; the structures themselves are large multistory, multiroom stone masonry apartments with many kivas. Pueblo Bonito, in Chaco Canyon, grew to a height of five stories containing more than eight hundred rooms and thirty-three kivas. The largest kivas in Chaco Canyon, called Great Kivas, became immense subterranean chambers. This period also saw the construction of spectacular cliff dwellings, the largest of which is Cliff Palace in Mesa Verde National Park in southwestern Colorado. But by the end of this period, all of the Anasazi settlements in the Four Corners region had been abandoned.

Why the Anasazi abandoned their homeland—their pueblos, their extensive water irrigation and storage facilities, their fields, and their elaborate network of roads—has been an intriguing mystery. While it was once assumed that a fifty-year drought destroyed the great Anasazi civilization, archaeologists have recently discounted this theory. A number of theories have arisen in its place, including divisive religious upheavals and wars among the Anasazis themselves. Many archaeologists believe that the Anasazis did not abandon their homeland

in one sudden mass exodus; it occurred over a period of time, in small groups, until finally all were gone.

During the Pueblo IV period, from 1300 to 1540, the Anasazis migrated to the east to the valley of the Rio Grande, to the south to the Zuni region along the upper reaches of the Little Colorado River, and to the west to the Hopi mesas, as well as to other areas where their stay proved less enduring. Many archaeological sites dating from this era have been found along these migration routes. The Pueblo V period, from 1540 to 1850, saw a mix of Spanish and Mexican elements disrupt and modify Anasazi Culture. The Pueblo VI period, from 1850 to the present, concerns itself with contemporary Pueblo Indian culture.

Throughout the Four Corners region, six hundred years of wind-borne dust accumulated on the abandoned Anasazi pueblos. Roof beams decayed and upper stories collapsed. Gradually, the desert reclaimed the landscape. Here and there, portions of stone masonry structures could be seen, but the full extent of Anasazi life in the region lay beneath the sand or was hidden away on the sides of cliffs in remote canyons. Only within the last century has the full extent of Anasazi life in the region begun to be appreciated. It is a process that likely will require many more decades, perhaps centuries, before the achievements of Anasazi Culture can be fully appreciated.

— D. L. Birchfield

SEE ALSO:

Archaic Period; Basket Maker; Canyon de Chelly; Chaco Canyon; Cliff Dwellings; Hopi; Kiva; Mesa Verde; Navajo; Pueblo; Zuni.

SUGGESTED READINGS:

Acatos, Sylvio. *Pueblos: Prehistoric Indian Cultures of the Southwest.* New York: Facts On File, 1990.

Ferguson, William, and Arthur Rohn. *Anasazi Ruins of the Southwest in Color.* Albuquerque: University of New Mexico Press, 1987.

Noble, David. *Ancient Ruins in the Southwest.* Flagstaff, AZ: Northland Press, 1981.

Pike, Donald. *Anasazi: Ancient People of the Rock.* Palo Alto, CA: American West Publishing, 1974.

Warren, Scott. *Cities in the Sand.* San Francisco: Chronicle Books, 1992.

ANDERSON, WALLACE "MAD BEAR" (1927–)

Wallace "Mad Bear" Anderson, a Tuscarora born in 1927, was one of the most noted Native rights activists in the 1950s, before the general upsurge in Native self-determination efforts in the 1960s. Anderson later became active in international affairs, where he was a noted spokesman for Native sovereignty.

Anderson was born in Buffalo, New York, and raised on the Tuscarora Reservation near Niagara Falls. During World War II, he served in the U.S. Navy at Okinawa, and he later also served in Korea. Anderson became an activist after his request for a GI Bill loan to build a house on the Tuscarora Reservation was rejected.

In the late 1950s, Mad Bear became part of the tax resistance movement that continues today. Many Iroquois maintain that they live in sovereign nations and that they should not be forced to pay United States or New York State taxes. In 1957, Mad Bear began to lead protests against Iroquois payment of New York State income taxes. At the height of the protest, several hundred Akwesasne (St. Regis) Mohawks marched to the Massena, New York, state courthouse, where they burned summonses issued for unpaid taxes. In 1958, Anderson played a leading role in protests against the seizure of 1,383 acres (560 hectares) of Tuscarora land by the New York Power Authority for construction of a dam and reservoir. Anderson and other Iroquois deflated workers' tires and blocked surveyors' transits. When the Tuscaroras refused to sell the land, a force of about one hundred state troopers and police invaded their reservation. Anderson met the troopers and police with 150 nonviolent demonstrators who blocked their trucks by lying in the road.

In March 1959, Anderson was part of a group that declared their sovereignty at the Iroquois Six Nations Reserve in Brantford, Ontario. This reserve was the settlement established by Joseph Brant and his followers after the American Revolution. The declaration prompted an occupation of the reserve's council house by Royal Canadian Mounted Police.

During 1967, Anderson formed the North American Indian Unity Caravan, which traveled the United States for six years. The tour allowed him to observe firsthand that the type of activism he had pioneered was spreading nationwide. Anderson also opposed termination legislation—that is, the federal laws, first enacted in the 1930s, that formally ended the sovereign status of Indian nations. In the late 1960s, Anderson gathered opposition to termination legislation from 133 Native tribes and nations and carried the message to Washington, D.C. This effectively killed the last attempt of the U.S. government to buy out reservations. In 1969, he helped initiate the takeover of Alcatraz Island.

SEE ALSO:

Alcatraz Island, Occupation of ; American Indian Movement; Brant, Joseph; Iroquois Confederacy; Termination Policy; Tribal Sovereignty; Tuscarora.

ANIMAL PEOPLE

People of many tribes, including those of the Northwest, believed that before Indians were created, the world was inhabited by a race of animal people. In the mythology of the Okanagan, a tribe of British Columbia and Washington State, Old-One created the earth to be the Mother of all people. The soil was Mother Earth's flesh, the rocks her bones, the wind her breath, and the trees and grass her hair. Old-One took some of her soil flesh and rolled it into balls of mud to create the first beings of the world—the animal people. These beings looked like animals and had all of the characteristics of animals (the fish could swim and the birds could fly), yet they could also talk and act like people.

Animal people fished and hunted, lived in lodges, and even had chiefs and slaves. Gigantic in size, they possessed supernatural powers that let them change back and forth from animal to human form. Only the deer were real animals without any special powers. The last balls of mud were rolled into different beings from the first. These the Old-One shaped like people, and when she blew on them, they came alive. The first humans knew very little about how to survive, and their helplessness made them easy prey for the animal people. Unfortunately, many of the animal people were selfish and cruel monsters. Some were also very ignorant. While they had to hunt deer to survive (and were actually pretty good hunters), they couldn't always tell which creatures were deer and which were humans. As a result, they sometimes ate people by mistake.

Things got so bad for the humans that the Old-One finally sent Coyote to kill all the evil animal people and start teaching the Natives the best ways to do things. Northwest stories are filled with accounts of how Coyote did just that. But Coyote was not just a hero; he was also quite a trickster. Many of the stories tell about the pranks Coyote liked to play on both the animal people and the humans he was trying to help.

After some time passed, things suddenly changed for the animal people. Some stories say "the world turned over" or "the world turned inside out," but in any case, the evil animal people were suddenly shrunk to the size of animals today. At the same time, they lost all their supernatural powers and their ability to speak and act like humans. Not all the animal people had been evil, however. Coyote changed the good ones not into animals but into special human beings. These beings came to be revered as the Ancients, the ancestors of all of today's Native Americans.

SEE ALSO:
Coyote Stories; Creation Stories; Tricksters.

SUGGESTED READINGS:

Campbell, Joseph. *Historical Atlas of World Mythology.* Vols. 1, 2, & 3. New York: Harper & Row, 1988.

Coffer, William E. *Spirits of the Sacred Mountains: Creation Stories of the American Indian.* New York: Van Nostrand Reinhold Company, 1978.

Erdoes, Richard, and Alfonso Ortiz, eds. *American Indian Myths and Legends.* New York: Pantheon Books, 1984.

Gill, Sam D. *Native American Religions: An Introduction.* Belmont, CA: Wadsworth, 1982.

Hirschfelder, Arlene, and Paulette Molin. *Encyclopedia of Native American Religions.* New York: Facts On File, 1992.

ANISHINABE

SEE Ojibwe.

ANNUITIES

An annuity is a series of fixed payments made periodically by one party, called a "grantor," to another party, called an "annuitant." Annuities usually run for some limited time; however, some annuities are granted in perpetuity. This means that the grantor guarantees to provide the payments forever. An example of a limited term annuity would be if a bank guaranteed to pay you $500 every year for ten years if you paid them $4,000 right now. If the bank guaranteed you and your heirs $300 a year forever in exchange for your payment, then it would be a perpetual annuity.

Many people wrongly believe that Native American peoples and their tribes receive large payments "just because they are Indian." Though the U.S. government and the governments of various states have paid and continue to pay annuities to tribes and their members, these payments are made in exchange for something (usually land) taken from the tribe. The annuities were usually granted in a formal agreement, often in a treaty. Some of the earliest agreements included substantial perpetual annuities. Over time, however, this changed. As the power of the European colonists grew and that of the Native American tribes decreased, the tribes were often forced into unfavorable agreements. These later agreements overrode earlier agreements and specified either lump sum payments or limited term annuities. These payments were generally far below market value.

One of the few perpetual annuities still being paid was specified in Article VI of the Treaty with the Six Nations, 1794. Under this agreement, a payment of $4,500 worth of goods, including cloth, was to be divided among the Mohawk, Oneida, Onondaga, Cayuga, Seneca, and Tuscarora Nations—the six nations of the Iroquois Confederacy. Today, the federally recognized successors to these nations continue to receive what they call the "treaty cloth." Because no allowance was made for devaluation of currency, inflation of cloth prices, or the increases in population, this annuity amounts to a small patch of cloth worth less than a dollar for each member of these nations. In recent years, the federal government has tried to get these nations to accept the annuity in cash or receive a single lump sum in lieu of the annual treaty cloth, but this has been refused, in large part because of the symbolic importance of the cloth.

Closely related to annuities are leases and royalties. A lease is an agreement in which one party, called a "landlord" or "lessor," allows another party, called the "lessee," to possess and use some property in return for some payment made by the lessee, without turning over actual ownership. In a royalty agreement, the owner of a property allows another party the right to exploit resources (for example, mining for coal, cutting timber, or drilling for oil) on their property in return for some payment.

Native lands that have not been taken in previous agreements are frequently the subject of lease or royalty agreements, in which the U.S. government or private companies seek to use remaining Native land or exploit its resources. Lease and royalty agreements, like those involving annuities, were usually negotiated from a position of Native weakness compared to the power of the company or government, so their payments are normally below market value as well.

Despite this injustice, a few tribes like the Osages have received large sums of money because of their vast mineral wealth. It is perhaps the heyday of the Osage oil boom that generates the false notion of Indian wealth. Unfortunately, these resources eventually run out. Current Osage royalties, if split among all tribal members, would not be sufficient to live on. Today, tribal money is more likely to come from economic development like gaming than from annuities or royalties.

SEE ALSO:
Gaming; Iroquois Confederacy; Osage; Treaties, Indian–United States.

A colored photo of Apache leader James A. Garfield. By the time this picture was taken, sometime around 1899, Apache tribal lands in Oklahoma had been opened up to individual ownership—first to Apaches and later to white settlers.

APACHE

The Southwestern Athabascan language, sometimes called Apachean, has seven dialects: Navajo, Western Apache, Chiricahua, Mescalero, Jicarilla, Lipan, and Kiowa-Apache. The Athabascan language family has four branches: Northern Athabascan, Southwestern Athabascan, Pacific Coast Athabascan, and Eyak, a southeast Alaska isolate. The Athabascan language family is one of three families within the

Wickiups—traditional frame structures covered with matting made of bark or brush—dot this scene from the White Mountain Apache Reservation in Arizona.

Na-Dene language phylum, one of the most widely distributed language phyla in North America. (In addition to the Athabascan language family, the other two Na-Dene families, the Tlingit family and the Haida family, are language isolates in the far north, Tlingit in southeast Alaska, and Haida in British Columbia.)

Apaches are, relatively speaking, new arrivals in the Southwest. Athabascans are generally believed to have been among the last peoples to have crossed the land bridge believed by many to have connected Siberia and Alaska during the last interglacial epoch. Most members of the language family still reside in the far north. Exactly when the Apaches and Navajos began their migration southward is not known, but it is clear that they had not arrived in the Southwest before the end of the fourteenth century.

The Southwest was home to a number of flourishing civilizations—the Anasazi, the Mogollon, and the Hohokam, and others—until near the end of the fourteenth century. Those ancient peoples are now believed to have become the Papago (Tohono O'odham), Pima, and Pueblo peoples of the contemporary Southwest. Scholars at one time assumed that the arrival of the Apaches and Navajos played a role in the abandonment of those ancient centers of civilization. However, the reasons these cultures left the area are unknown. It may have been war among the ancient tribes or intense religious conflicts.

In any case, the Apaches and Navajos probably arrived to find that the Anasazis in the Four Corners area had reestablished themselves in what is now known as the Pueblo villages of the upper Rio Grande Valley in New Mexico. (The Four Corners area is where corners of Colorado, New Mexico, Arizona, and Utah come together in a point; the Navajo Nation makes its home in that area in the states of New Mexico, Arizona, and Utah.)

The Mogollons in southwestern New Mexico and southeastern Arizona and the Hohokams in southern Arizona had likewise migrated from their ancient ruins. When Spaniards first entered the region, with the expedition of Francisco de Coronado in 1540, the Apaches and Navajos had already established themselves throughout their homeland.

The Grand Apacheria, as it was known, the homeland of the Apache, was a vast region stretching from central Arizona in the west to central and south Texas in the east, and from northern Mexico in the south to the High Plains of eastern Colorado in the north. This region was divided between Eastern and Western Apaches. Eastern Apaches were Plains Apaches. In the days before the horse, and before the historic southward migration of the Comanche Nation in the early 1700s, the Plains Apaches were the lords of the southern Plains. Western Apaches lived primarily on the western side of the continental divide in the mountains of Arizona and western New Mexico. When

the Comanches adopted the use of the horse and migrated southward out of Wyoming, they displaced the Eastern Apaches from the southern Great Plains, who then took up residence in the mountainous country of eastern New Mexico.

Apaches have endured severe disruptions of their economic and political life, first by the Spanish, then by the Comanches, and later by the United States. Apaches became known to the Spanish as a result of a number of Spanish exploratory expeditions into the Southwest during the sixteenth century, beginning with the Coronado expedition of 1540 and including a number of others, at intervals, throughout the century. (Some of these expeditions were authorized by the Spanish colonial powers; others were unauthorized forays into Indian land and were therefore, technically illegal.) It was not until 1598, however, that Apaches had to adjust to the presence of Europeans within their homeland, when the colonizing expedition of Juan de Oñate entered the Pueblo country of the upper

A calf roper at the White Mountain Apache Rodeo in Arizona.

A Jicarilla Apache ceremonial race. The Jicarilla Apache Reservation is in north-central New Mexico.

Rio Grande Valley of the present state of New Mexico, with the intention of establishing a permanent Spanish colony. The Oñate expedition successfully colonized New Mexico, and by 1610, the town of Santa Fe had been founded.

Until the arrival of the Spanish, the Apaches and the Pueblos had enjoyed a trading relationship. Pueblos traded their agricultural products and pottery to the Apaches for buffalo robes and dried meat. The annual visits of entire Apache tribes for trade fairs with the Pueblos, primarily at the pueblos of Taos and Pícuris, were described with awe by the early Spaniards in the region. The Spanish, however, began to confiscate the Pueblo trade surpluses annually, thereby disrupting the trade. Nonetheless, some Apaches, notably the Jicarillas, became friends and allies of the Spanish.

The historic southward migration of the Comanche Nation, beginning around 1700, was devastating for the Eastern Apaches. By about 1725, the Comanches had established authority throughout the whole of the southern Plains region, pushing the Eastern Apaches (the Jicarillas north of Santa Fe and the Mescaleros south of Santa Fe) into the mountains of the front range of the Rockies in New Mexico. Denied access to the buffalo herds, the Apaches turned to Spanish cattle and horses as a substitute. When the Spanish were able to conclude a treaty of peace with the Comanches in 1786, they employed large bodies of Comanche and Navajo auxiliary troops, with Spanish regulars, in implementing an Apache policy that pacified the entire Southwestern frontier by 1790. Each individual Apache group was hunted down and cornered, then offered a subsidy sufficient for their maintenance if they would settle near a Spanish mission, refrain from raiding Spanish livestock, and live peacefully. One by one, each Apache group accepted the terms. The peace, though little studied by modern scholars, is thought to have endured until near the end of the Spanish colonial era. (For how the peace was achieved, see *The Apache Frontier*, by Max Moorhead.)

In the 1820s, the Mexican Revolution disrupted the peace, and when the United States moved into the Southwest at the end of the Mexican–American War in the mid-1800s, the Apaches resisted the intrusion. The United States, lacking Spanish diplomatic skills, the Spanish language, and Spanish understanding of the Apaches, sought to subjugate the Apaches militarily, an undertaking that was not achieved until the final surrender of Geronimo's band in 1886. Some Apaches became prisoners of war, shipped first to Florida, then to Alabama, and finally to Oklahoma. Others entered a period of desultory reservation life in the Southwest.

Federally recognized contemporary Apache tribal governments are located in Arizona, New Mexico, and Oklahoma. Apache reservations are also located in Arizona and New Mexico. But in Oklahoma, Apache tribal land was made available for individual ownership—first to Apaches and then to non-Indian settlers, who swarmed into Native lands—under the General Allotment Act of 1887, also known as the Dawes Act, and Oklahoma Apaches became citizens of the new state of Oklahoma, and of the United States, in 1907. Apaches in Arizona and New Mexico were not granted United States citizenship until 1924.

Members of the Gaan dance group at the San Carlos Apache Reservation in Arizona.

After attempting to terminate its governmental relationship with Indian tribes in the 1950s, the United States has since adopted a policy of assisting the tribes in achieving some measure of self-determination, and the United States Supreme Court has upheld some attributes of sovereignty for Indian nations. In recent years, for example, Apache enterprises under tribal authority, such as

An Apache delegate to the parliament of the World's Religions in Chicago, August 1993, listens to opening remarks as other delegates, attired in less traditional clothing, give him and his regalia a wide berth.

ski areas, resorts, and lumber mills, have helped alleviate chronically high rates of unemployment on the reservations. Bilingual and bicultural educational programs have resulted from direct Apache involvement in the educational process, something that was denied to them until recently.

For the Apaches, the family is the primary unit of political as well as cultural life. Apaches have never been a unified nation politically, and individual Apache tribes, until very recently, have never had a centralized government of any kind, traditional or otherwise. Extended family groups acted entirely independently of one another. At intervals during the year, a number of these family groups, related by dialect, custom, intermarriage, and geographical proximity, might come together as conditions and circumstances might warrant. As a whole, these groups might be identifiable as a tribal division, but they almost never acted together as a tribal division or as a nation, not even when faced with the overwhelming threat of the Comanche migration into their southern Plains

territory. The existence of these many different independent extended family groups of Apaches made it impossible for Spain, Mexico, or the United States to forge treaties with the Apache Nation as a whole. Each group had to be treated individually, an undertaking that proved difficult for each colonizer who attempted to establish authority within the Apache homeland. Finally, the United States was able to assert its authority over the Southwest through overwhelming numbers and concentrated effort.

Apache culture is matrilineal. Once married, the man goes with the wife's extended family, where she is surrounded by her relatives. Spousal abuse is practically unknown in such a system. Should the marriage not endure, child custody quarrels are also unknown. The children remain with the wife's extended family. Marital harmony is encouraged by a custom forbidding the mother of the wife to speak to, or even be in the presence of, her son-in-law. No such stricture applies to the grandmother of the wife, who frequently is a powerful presence in family life. Apache women play important roles in the culture as a whole, and children are deeply loved.

Apaches have adhered strongly to their culture in the face of overwhelming attempts to suppress it, while at the same time being adaptable. The most enduring Apache custom is the girl's puberty ceremony each summer. Clan relatives still play important roles in these ceremonies, when girls become Changing Woman for four days. These are spectacular public events, which are proudly and vigorously advertised by the tribe.

Many Apache children were sent to Carlisle Indian School, in Pennsylvania, not long after the school was founded in 1879 by Richard Henry Pratt, a large group of them arriving in 1887. Government and mission schools were established among the Apaches in the 1890s. These schools vigorously pursued policies aimed at forcing Apache children to assimilate into the dominant culture, including instruction only in English. By 1952, 80 percent of the Apaches in Arizona spoke English.

Today, Apaches participate in decisions involving the education of their young, and this has resulted in exemplary bilingual and bicultural programs at the public schools at both the San Carlos and Fort Apache Reservations, especially in the elementary grades. In 1959, the Jicarillas incorporated their school district with the surrounding Hispanic towns. Within thirty years, its school board included four Jicarilla members, including the editor of the tribal newspaper. In 1988, the Jicarilla school district was chosen New Mexico School District of the Year.

Some Apache communities, like the Cibecue community at White Mountain Reservation, are more conservative and traditional than other Apache communities, but all Apache communities value their traditional culture, which has proven to be enduring. Apaches also value education. The Camp Verde Reservation has the highest percentage of its young people enrolled in college of any Arizona tribe. Increasingly, especially in communities such as the White Mountain Reservation, education is being used as a tool to develop human resources so that the educated tribal members can find ways for the tribe to engage in economic activity. This will allow more of its people to remain on the reservation, thus preserving its community and culture.

The winner of a Miss Rodeo Apache contest at the White Mountain Apache Rodeo smiles from beneath her hat.

Apaches were granted United States citizenship under the Indian Citizenship Act of 1924. They did not legally acquire the right to practice their Native religion until the passage of the American Indian Religious Freedom Act of 1978. Other important rights, and some attributes of sovereignty, have been restored to them by such legislation as the Indian Civil Rights Act of 1966, the Indian Self-Determination and Educational Assistance Act of 1975, and the Indian Child Welfare Act of 1978.

— D. L. Birchfield

SEE ALSO:

Anasazi; Arizona; Camp Verde Reservation; Carlisle Indian School; Cochise; Coronado Expedition; Dawes Commission; Fort Apache Reservation; General Allotment Act; Geronimo; Hohokam; Jicarilla Apache; Mescalero Apache; Mexican-American War; Mogollon Culture; Navajo; New Mexico; New Spain; Oklahoma; Oñate Expedition; Pima; Pueblo; San Carlos Reservation; Self-determination Policy; Spain; Termination Policy; Tohono O'odham; Tribal Sovereignty.

SUGGESTED READINGS:

Bushkirk, Winfred. *The Western Apache*. Norman: University of Oklahoma Press, 1986.

Forbes, Jack D. *Apache, Navaho, and Spaniard*. Norman: The University of Oklahoma Press, 1969 and 1994.

Melody, Michael E. *The Apaches: A Critical Bibliography*. Bloomington: Indiana University Press, 1977.

Moorhead, Max. *The Apache Frontier*. Norman: University of Oklahoma Press, 1968.

Perry, Richard J. *Apache Reservation: Indigenous Peoples and the American State*. Austin: University of Texas Press, 1993.

Sonnichsen, C. L. *The Mescalero Apaches*. 2d ed. Norman: University of Oklahoma Press, 1973.

APES, WILLIAM (1798–c. 1839)

William Apes, a Pequot who lived from 1798 to approximately 1839, was a direct descendant of the Wampanoag war chief Metacom (known to the English as King Philip). Apes was an ordained Methodist preacher who shared with Metacom a seething hatred for the way Euro-Americans treated his people. In 1836, 160 years after Metacom was killed, then drawn and quartered, Apes delivered a passionate eulogy for him on Federal Street in Boston. His speech ended with a paraphrased quote from the Puritan religious leader, Dr. Increase Mather. In the original speech, Mather had bid God to come to the Puritans' aid in their pursuit of Metacom. In his speech, Apes said, "Nor could they, the Pilgrims, cease crying to the Lord against [King] Philip, until they had prayed the bullet through his heart. If this is the way they pray, that is bullets through people's hearts, I hope they will *not* pray for me; I should rather be excused."

Shortly after this speech, Apes disappeared from public view at the age of thirty-eight and was never heard from again. Speculation was that he was murdered, but the circumstances of Apes's death have been lost to history. Apes authored the books *Eulogy on King Philip* (1836), *Increase of the Kingdom of Christ* (1831), and *A Son of the Forest* (1831). His papers are collected in *On Our Own Ground: The Complete Writings of William Apes, a Pequot*, edited by Barry O'Connell (University of Massachusetts Press, 1992).

SEE ALSO:

King Philip; Wampanoag.

AQUASH, ANNA MAE PICTOU (1945–1976)

Anna Mae Pictou was a Micmac from Nova Scotia, Canada. She attended Wheelock College in Massachusetts and had dreamed of assembling a cultural history on American Indians. In 1969, she helped organize the Boston Indian Council, which was used to help Native American alcoholics.

In 1970, she was exposed to the American Indian Movement (AIM) when AIM organizer Russell Means attended a Thanksgiving demonstration in Boston. She participated in the Trail of Broken Treaties and the occupation of Wounded Knee. While at Wounded Knee, Anna Mae married her friend Nogeeshik Aquash, an Ojibwe (Chippewa) artist. She also helped dig bunkers, participated in nightly patrols, and slipped in and out of the village to obtain supplies for the warriors.

After Wounded Knee, Anna Mae Aquash set up Indian cultural showings at the National Arts Centre. She and Nogeeshik Aquash separated, and she went to St. Paul, Minnesota, where she taught at the Red School House survival school.

At one time, during a period when the FBI was known to be infiltrating AIM with agents whose job was to stir up trouble and suspicion among the members, some Indians suspected Anna Mae Aquash of being an infiltrator of AIM for the government. Although her peers within AIM were satisfied that she was not an informant, she still had to live under the watchful eyes of others. Throughout the early and mid-1970s, Aquash expressed the wish that, should anything happen to her, her children be told that she lived—and died—in service to her people.

On February 24, 1976, Anna Mae Aquash was found dead on the Pine Ridge Reservation, at thirty years of age. She was wearing a distinctive turquoise ring and bracelet. The bracelet was turned over to the Federal Bureau of Investigation. Her body was not identified at that time, even though some of the investigators had had dealings with her previously.

The cause of her death was ruled as exposure, and her hands were cut off at the wrists and sent to Washington, D.C., for identification. She was buried as "Jane Doe" on March 2 and identified the day after. Her family was notified and requested an exhumation of the body and a second autopsy. The second autopsy revealed that Anna Mae had been executed at point-blank range from a .38 handgun in the back of the head.

Two grand jury investigations have taken place since Anna Mae's murder, and a third was under way in 1994. Speculation is that a Native, possibly working for the government at a time of great conflict at Pine Ridge, took the life of the young woman. The effect of the life and work of Anna Mae Aquash on the people closest to her within the Indian movement is captured by her friend Mary Brave Bird Crow Dog in *Lakota Woman*, by Mary Crow Dog with Richard Erdoes (published in paperback in 1990 by HarperCollins, New York.)

SEE ALSO:
American Indian Movement; Crow Dog, Mary; Means, Russell; Trail of Broken Treaties; Wounded Knee, Confrontation at (1973).

ARAPAHO

The Arapahos were known in their earliest history as the Bison Path People because they followed the buffalo on the northern Plains. The name *Arapaho* may have derived from a Pawnee word meaning "trader," or it may have come from a Siouan Crow term that means "tattooed people," which is what the Blackfeet called the Arapahos. The Arapahos did not come up with the name themselves since they do not even have an *r* sound in their language. The Arapahos call themselves "Our People" and speak a dialect of Algonquian, one of the few western tribes to do so.

Some theories place the Arapahos in northern Minnesota before moving onto the Plains. But for the most part, it is believed that the Arapahos have long lived on the northern Plains. At some point in their history—also in their ancient stories—the Arapahos split into the Southern and Northern Arapahos. Their legends tell of crossing a great river, the Missouri, when the ice cracked and split the Northern and Southern Arapahos. They wandered freely from the Cheyenne River into eastern Colorado and from the Rockies into the Black Hills. They camped in winter near clear water streams along the eastern Rockies and ventured as far as western Nebraska and Kansas during buffalo hunts.

The Arapahos had age-graded societies; as they grew older, boys entered one society and then another. One of their most important religious ceremonies was the Sun Dance. Over the days of this ritual, they asked for nature to continue to give its gifts and allow the tribe to prosper. The societies each had their role in the Sun Dance, performing complex rituals around a sacred tree trunk. Tribal members often went without food or sleep for days during the ceremony. Their most sacred object was a flat pipe that was used only on special ceremonial occasions.

The Arapahos became closely allied with the Cheyennes after meeting that nation in the Black Hills. The Cheyennes needed the Arapahos as allies against their foe, the Crows, and the Arapahos needed the Cheyennes to help in trade along the Missouri River.

The Arapahos believed that their Creator, the Man-Above, had created the Rocky Mountains as a barrier to separate them from their enemies. To the east were the Pawnees and to the south the Comanches and Kiowas; all three had less than friendly relations with the Arapahos. The Arapahos fought against the Crows and also with the Utes and Shoshones in the mountains to the west.

The Arapahos were known for their trading skills and began acquiring horses in the late 1700s and early 1800s. They would obtain the horses either through barter or through raids conducted on villages and on small roving bands of people. Yet they rarely encountered or were seen by Europeans.

On September 8, 1851, a designated council took place between the Plains Nations and the United States government. The superintendent of Indian affairs, David D. Mitchell, addressed the Arapaho, Cheyenne, Crow, and Sioux chiefs, explaining the wishes of the Washington, D.C., bureaucrats. Mitchell told them they would be compensated for the grass eaten by the settlers' cattle and the devastation of the buffalo. The president of the United States wanted the right for settlers to travel the roads to the west without threat and also wanted to build forts to protect them. Mitchell told them that certain lands would be designated as tribal lands or reservations.

The Arapahos, along with the Cheyennes, were assigned a territory between the Platte and Arkansas Rivers. The treaty called for lasting peace, the right of the federal government to build posts, punishment for raids, specific boundaries but open fishing and hunting rights, and the payment of annuities of $50,000 in goods for fifty years. The latter was reduced to $15,000 later without the knowledge or consent of the Indian nations. The agreement sounded good to the chiefs, who wanted peaceful relations with the settlers.

But other problems remained. Eastern Native American nations were being forced into Arapaho territory and were hunting game in land that the Arapahos had settled. In addition, around 1858, Arapaho land was being overrun by gold miners. Towns and villages were being erected on Native land without regard to the landowners.

In February 1861, the Southern Arapahos signed a treaty with the federal government, ceding all their lands except a reservation tract in eastern Colorado. Six years later, the Medicine Lodge Council of 1867 led the Southern Arapahos into Oklahoma (then called Indian Territory). Arapaho chief Little Raven discussed the treaty obligations with his nation as they met on the Medicine

A rendering of an Arapaho Ghost Dance, done around 1900. The Southern Arapahos learned of the Ghost Dance faith from Sitting Bull, a Southern Arapaho leader who had brought word of it into Indian Territory (present-day Oklahoma) from the northern Plains.

A group of Arapaho Indians participate in a ceremony restoring the remains and sacred objects of their ancestors to their rightful burial place. Restorations like this are occurring following decades of sacred sites being disturbed by curiosity seekers and scientists alike.

Lodge River in Kansas. This treaty gave the Arapahos and Cheyennes a tract of land located in the Cherokee Outlet in what is now Oklahoma along the Kansas state line and along the Osage Reservation line to the east. The two nations mistakenly settled on the wrong land, and when the mistake was acknowledged, they asked for a different reservation. They cited poor soil and the lack of woodlands and water as reasons for wanting a different reservation. The Arapahos and Cheyennes were jointly assigned a new reservation along the North Canadian and Washita Rivers by presidential proclamation in August 1869. The Arapaho school opened in 1870 and continued to run as a boarding school until 1908, when it consolidated with the Cheyenne school.

Because of Northern Arapaho resistance, it took longer for the federal government to settle this tribe on a reservation. The Northern Arapahos were living in the Powder River country, clinging to their land. There were occasional clashes between Native peoples and non-Native invaders.

The Arapahos were at the Little Bighorn when General George Custer and all his troops were annihilated during an attack on a Sioux, Cheyenne, and Arapaho encampment. The date was June 25, 1875. The three nations split into their separate bands and celebrated their victory.

Following Custer's defeat at the Little Bighorn, the United States Army staged a winter invasion on the Powder River country, tearing up winter camps and harassing the Natives. The Arapahos finally surrendered at Camp Robinson, where they stayed for a year as prisoners of war.

Although the Shoshones had been the enemy of the Arapahos, they took pity on the Arapahos and gave them temporary refuge in 1878. The U.S. government accepted this as a permanent settlement. The two nations still live on the Wind River Reservation together. However, in 1927, the Shoshones took their case to the Court of Claims and were paid for the appraised value of half their land, which they have had to share with the Arapahos. Although the two nations are no longer enemies, they still hold themselves apart from one another.

In 1890, the Southern Arapahos helped spread the word of the Ghost Dance religion to other Indian Territory nations. A Southern Arapaho named Sitting Bull had lived among the Northern Arapahos and had come back to the reservation in Indian Territory. He spread the word of an Indian messiah and the reunion of Indian people on a rejuvenated earth.

During the height of the Ghost Dance religion, the Dawes Commission sought to buy Arapaho reservation land and allot land to Native individuals and then open up the remaining lands to non-Indians. April 19, 1892, marked the day that Arapaho and Cheyenne land was opened up for non-Native settlement.

Under provisions of the Oklahoma Indian Welfare Act of 1936, the Cheyenne and Arapaho Nations joined in creating a constitution and by-laws and reorganized their governments. They organized the Cheyenne-Arapaho Business Committee, which consists of seven Arapaho and seven Cheyenne members. Committee members are elected every two years by popular vote; the committee is headquartered in Concho, Oklahoma.

For the most part, the Arapahos have been Christianized, taking on the Protestant faith. However, there are a number of Arapahos who are Mennonite and others who are members of the Native American Church.

In recent decades, the Arapahos have been involved in numerous battles to retain control over their land and resources. In 1977, the Arapahos became involved in water rights disputes. They, along with other Native nations, were fighting through the federal court system to retain their water rights or to get back that which had been taken from them. In the 1980s, thievery of large amounts of Indian oil was detected on the Wind River Reservation. The Arapahos and Shoshones leased part of their land to different oil companies but a lack of governmental monitoring allowed the companies to take advantage of the two nations.

Events such as these have taken the Arapahos and many other nations into the federal courts, the new arena for the continuation of Indian wars.

— S. S. Davis

SEE ALSO:
Algonquian; Black Hills; Cheyenne; Comanche; Crow; Custer, George Armstrong; Dawes Commission; General Allotment Act; Ghost Dance Religion; Kiowa; Little Bighorn, Battle of the; Oklahoma; Osage; Shoshone; Siouan Nations; Sitting Bull; Ute.

SUGGESTED READINGS:

Debo, Angie. *A History of the Indians of the United States.* Norman: University of Oklahoma Press, 1970.

Deloria, Vine, Jr. *Custer Died for Your Sins.* New York: Macmillan, 1969.

Josephy, Alvin M., Jr. *Now That the Buffalo's Gone.* Norman: University of Oklahoma Press, 1982.

Lazarus, Edward. *Black Hills, White Justice.* New York: HarperCollins Publishers, 1991.

Wright, Muriel H. *A Guide to the Indian Tribes of Oklahoma.* Norman: University of Oklahoma Press, 1951.

ARAWAK

The Arawaks are a group of culturally diverse Indian peoples who inhabit the tropical forests of Columbia, Venezuela, Guyana, French Guiana, Surinam, Bolivia, and Peru. Before the time of Columbus, Arawakan tribes covered an area from Florida to Paraguay and from the Andes Mountains to the Atlantic Ocean. It is estimated that only fifty different Arawakan cultures still exist.

Before the Spanish conquest in 1540, one of these Arawakan groups migrated north to the Caribbean and settled on the islands of the Bahamas, the Greater Antilles, and Trinidad. This group, which called themselves the Tainos, established a highly developed and politically organized culture based on agriculture, fishing, and the hunting of sea mammals.

Where land was fertile—along the lower Amazon, for example, on the islands of the Caribbean Sea, and along the coast of Brazil—both mainland and island Arawakan communities were large (often two thousand people or more) and consisted of multifamily households holding as many as fifty people each. They practiced a system of raising root plants called *conuco*, where they burned forest areas, formed mounds out of the rich ash, and then planted bitter yuca, yams, peanuts, and other root plants, as well as peppers, corn, beans, tobacco, squash, and even pineapples. For protein, Arawakans caught iguanas, pigeons, parrots, snakes, worms, spiders, shellfish, fish, crabs, turtles, and, where available, sea mammals such as the manatee, or sea cow.

Because of the warm climate, the Arawaks did not have to build elaborate housing or gather fuel for heating. Food was so abundant and easy to harvest that they had the leisure time to design and make superbly crafted pottery, baskets, woven cotton cloth, and elaborate stone sculptures. Both men and women painted their bodies and ornamented them with jewelry of gold, stone, bone, and shell. The Arawaks fermented alcoholic drinks and smoked a primitive kind of cigar. They also enjoyed ball games, informal feasts, dances, and elaborate religious ceremonies.

Arawaks have been described as a peaceful, gentle, and friendly people. Villages were governed by headmen chosen from the leaders of its multi-family households. An Arawakan territory was typically run by a chief, although large territories were often subdivided into statelike provinces that were governed by subchiefs. Arawakan religious systems were also highly organized, with priests or shamans who wielded control with their ability to capture good and evil spirits inside statues they called *zemis*. Arawakans believed that the plants they harvested and the animals they hunted were manifestations of the gods to which they prayed, given to them as gifts for which they must express their thanks.

The Spanish conquest of 1540 had a devastating effect on Arawakan cultures. Those people who were not killed outright died as Spanish slaves or from the epidemic diseases the Spanish brought with them from Europe.

The mainland cultures did not fare much better. Their advanced agricultural practices, large villages, most of their political and social structure, their mounds and temples, even much of their intricate design work, all but disappeared at the hands of the conquistadores. Today, most Arawakans hunt, fish, and practice a sort of slash-and-burn farming. They now live in small communities of between one hundred and two hundred people. They weave simple cloth and make only plain pots. Although most of their religious rites and practices have been forgotten, some remain.

SEE ALSO:

Cacique; Caribbean, Indigenous Cultures of; Columbus, Christopher; Spain; Taino.

ARCHAIC PERIOD

The term *Archaic* is generally used by archaeologists to designate Native American cultures that existed between 8000 B.C.E. and 1250 C.E. The period is also sometimes called the "Golden Age of Archaeology."

The general consensus in academic archaeology late in the twentieth century holds that North America was first peopled by a series of migrations from Asia that occurred sometime during the Pleistocene Era, a period of recurring ice ages seventy-five thousand to eight thousand years ago. During this time, much of North America's northern half was covered from time to time by advancing and then retreating layers of ice. During the ice ages, weather patterns along the eastern side of the western mountains that run roughly north-northwest to south-southeast along the western spine of North America generally kept deep ice from forming on the High Plains. The westward movement of storms caused copious snows to form glaciers on the higher mountains, robbing the air of moisture on their eastern sides. These glaciers formed a corridor that is supposed to have served as a conduit for the Asian migrants who are said to have spread across the Western Hemisphere.

The same weather patterns produced areas (such as the high plateau of Nevada) that, though deserts today, had a milder, cooler, wetter climate that allowed game animals to flourish. These included several types of mammoths (some as large as present-day African elephants) and primordial bison (who also were larger than later types), all of them living in an environment that ranged from swamps to dense forests to lush grasslands.

By eleven thousand years ago, Native artifacts became more widespread, more easily identified, and more technologically advanced, thus, the emphasis on the Folsom, Clovis, and Plano (or Plainview) points, all of which were first found at sites in present-day New Mexico and Texas. Each dates to between 10,000 and 5000 B.C.E. The Clovis points seem to be the oldest, dating to about 12,000 B.C.E., with Folsom points dating to 8000 B.C.E., and Plano points recognizable at 7500 to 4500 B.C.E. Each type of point is used to identify the culture that used it.

Even by 9000 B.C.E., different cultures were evolving. For example, the Cascade (or "Old Cordilleran") style of point was being used in the Pacific Northwest. Its design differed slightly from the Folsom points used in other areas. Similarly, a distinct culture was evolving at this time in some areas of the Great Basin, Arizona, and Utah; today, these peoples usually are called the Desert Cultures. Even five thousand to seven thousand years ago, examples of very distinct cultures arise, such as the Copper Culture of present-day Wisconsin, in which people forged lance points and other articles from the copper common to the region. This was one of the earliest metalworking cultures in the world.

More recently than 5000 B.C.E., individual cultures are perhaps best discussed on their own in most cases. Generally, a drier and warmer climate, as well as technological advances, allowed many Native cultures to move away from hunting as a sole means of survival; Native peoples began to forage and gather food. This eventually led to domesticating plants and animals, as well as other forms of sedentary agriculture and (in some cases) civilizations with large urban concentrations of population supported by forms of agriculture, which present-day scholars are still rediscovering.

SEE ALSO:

Clovis Culture; Culture Areas of North America; Folsom Culture.

ARCHITECTURE, INDIAN

Before Europeans arrived in the Americas (the so-called New World), Indian civilizations flourished and built tremendous city complexes, temples, pyramids, roads, and huge earthen mounds. These structures equaled or surpassed those built in Europe—the so-called Old World. The rise of agriculture in the Americas enabled indigenous people to build large

This ancient Mexican architecture features representations of the Aztec-Toltec figure Quetzalcoatl. These figures are from Teotihuacán.

Calle Hatunrumiyoc, a street built along a remarkably preserved Inca wall in Cuzco, the ancient Inca capital that is now a part of Peru.

structures. Agricultural societies are more stable and have higher populations and greater wealth than hunter-gatherer societies, which need to be more mobile. Hunter-gatherer societies also had to construct buildings that could easily be moved or left for a season. Agricultural communities were found throughout the Western Hemisphere in South America, Mesoamerica (present-day Central America and southern Mexico), and North America.

In South America, monumental architecture developed primarily along the west coast, in what are now the countries of Ecuador, Bolivia, Peru, and Chile. The land along the coast is a very dry desert that rises quickly to form the steep Andes Mountains. Agriculture is thought to have developed in this area around the fifth century B.C.E. With agriculture came a larger, more stable population and the development of cities and architecture.

In the pre-Inca period (before 1400 C.E.), one of the first major public buildings was a terraced temple-pyramid at Chuquitanta, Peru. Other cities were also built, usually with terraced platforms or pyramids built around a central plaza.

The Chavins (1000–300 B.C.E.) were the first to employ a unified style of architecture. The main center of this culture was the city of Chavin de Huantar. The site has stepped masonry platforms, terraces, and sunken plazas. During the Huari Empire (600–1000 C.E.), the large city of Huari was built with plazas, large buildings, and homes. The period from 1000 to 1475 C.E. was characterized by groups of local states and cities, each with its own monumental architecture.

The Inca Empire (1438–1532 C.E.) was named for what these people called their king, the Inca. This is the Indian group that the Spanish conquistador Francisco Pizarro encountered when he arrived in South America. (The Inca Empire was centralized and dependent upon the leadership of its ruler, the Inca himself. It was his kidnapping by the Spanish conquerors, and subsequent holding of him for ransom, that preceded Spain's coming to rule the entire area.)

The Incas were famous for their architectural and engineering skills and drew upon the knowledge of all of the kingdoms that had preceded them in building their architecture. Their primary build-

The Temple of Caana, a site at the Caracol Maya ruins.

ing materials were massive stones that were cut and sanded until they fit tightly together. The stones were so big that it could take many laborers to move even one. They did not use mortar in their stone walls, some of which are still in perfect condition. Even today, a knife blade will not fit between the stones. They built walls, temples, city complexes, and gateways. The Incas were also famous for their extensive system of roads, which extended thousands of miles (kilometers) from Ecuador to Chile. They built terraces into the steep mountainsides so that the land could be cultivated.

The capital of the Incas was Cuzco, but the best preserved of their cities is Machu Picchu, a city on a remote mountaintop that was lost and forgotten until it was discovered by the explorer Hiram Bingham in 1911.

In the region known as Mesoamerica, which includes the countries of Belize, Nicaragua, El Salvador, Honduras, Guatemala, and Mexico, architectural achievement excelled. During the period from 1200 B.C.E. to 300 B.C.E. on the Gulf Coast of Mexico, a civilization known as the Olmec developed. The Olmec Indians built large religious centers of stone that included temples, pyramids, and

the homes of the elite. The Olmec architectural style diffused throughout Mesoamerica and was visible in the cities of Monte Albán and early Maya centers.

The Mayas of the Classic Period (100–900 C.E.) lived in the dense jungles of Central America, including Guatemala, Nicaragua, Honduras, and the Yucatán Peninsula in southern Mexico, and their descendants still live there today. The Mayas were famous for their knowledge of math and astronomy. They inherited and adapted architectural styles from the Olmecs and other Mesoamerican cultures, building large cities with temples, observatories, palaces, monasteries, and baths.

Mayan pyramids were very steep, and the Mayas had temples on top for religious observances. The pyramids also often had a shaft that went deep inside and led to an underground burial chamber. The Mayas were the first in the Americas to build using corbelled vaults, walls that slope inward and are topped by a keystone. Later in their civilization, the Mayas, influenced by tribes to the north, built ceremonial ball courts. These ball courts had a special religious significance to the cultures that built them and may have been used for ritual warfare.

The cultures of central Mexico that developed after the Olmecs and before the Aztecs were responsible for the creation of numerous important cities and religious centers. The great cities of Teotihuacán and Monte Albán flourished during what is known as the Classic Period (200 to 700 C.E.). The city of Teotihuacán, located northeast of Mexico City, had a total population of two hundred thousand people by the sixth century C.E. and was larger than ancient Rome. The city had long avenues along which were located enormous pyramids, a marketplace, palaces, and mansions. The largest pyramids were the Temple of the Sun and the Temple of the Moon. These pyramids were flat on top and built in multiple levels, with a rectangular panel with raised borders placed above each sloping level. The architectural style of Teotihuacán became so famous it spread in all directions.

The city of Monte Albán, located in the Mexican state of Oaxaca, sat on a mountaintop overlooking a valley. Built in the form of a large rectangle, it had pyramids and palaces, as well.

The Mixteca-Puebla peoples built a pyramid at Cholula. It measures 186 feet (56.5 meters) high and 900 feet (273 meters) on each side. It is the largest structure ever built by American Indians. Like many of the pyramids of Mesoamerica, it was formed by larger pyramids being built over smaller ones.

The Toltecs (900 to 1200 C.E.) were master architects and builders, drawing upon all of the architectural heritage that had preceded them. Their traditions spread south to the Maya and as far north as the cultures along the Mississippi in North America. The Toltecs' cities included pillared halls, ornamental pyramids, and masonry ball courts. Their most famous city was Tula.

The Aztecs ruled much of Mexico from 1325 to 1519. A warlike nation, they invaded the Toltec Empire from the north and built a city called Tenochtitlán in a swampy area in the central mountain valley of Mexico. Built upon a lake, the city had a system of canals, and transportation was by boat. There were several large pyramids, a marketplace, and temples. When the Spanish arrived, the city had a population of approximately two

An ancient Mixtec ceremonial center at Mitla, near present-day Oaxaca, Mexico.

hundred thousand people. Most of what was once Tenochtitlán has sunk and now lies buried beneath Mexico City, a city of more than fifteen and a half million people today.

In what is today the United States, there were two major culture areas that produced monumental architecture, the remains of which can still be seen. These were the Mound Builders and the Indians of the Southwest. These Indians, like the Mesoamericans, were farmers, and the development of their large-scale architecture coincided with the introduction of the hoe and maize from Mexico. Their architecture had several features in common with the architecture of Mexico, including pyramids and ball courts. The Mound Builders' pyramids, although built of earth, were as large as many in Mexico and had the same flat tops. As in Mexico, the pyramids were often enlarged by building one over the other.

In what is now the state of Illinois, right across the Mississippi River from St. Louis, are the remains of an ancient city that was larger than London—Cahokia. Cahokia served as a trade center among Indians from the Atlantic to the Pacific Oceans, north to Canada and south to Mexico. The major architectural feature of the city was an enormous pyramid of earth. Known as Monk's Mound, the pyramid covers a total of sixteen acres (six hectares). It was built by people carrying baskets full of earth and then dumping them one on top of another.

There were many other smaller earthen mounds at Cahokia and a rectangular open plaza. Archaeologists have also discovered the remains of an ancient calendar like Stonehenge, but built of wood. We know little about the Indians who built the city of Cahokia, which had been abandoned by the time Europeans arrived. Cahokia is the largest of the Mound Builder cities, but Indian tribes throughout the southeastern United States and along the Mississippi River built earthen mounds and had city organizations similar to that of Cahokia.

Indians of the present-day U.S. Southwest also built impressive city structures. Those who lived in and built the cities of Mesa Verde and the settlement at Chaco Canyon are known as the Anasazi, or the "Ancient Ones." Their culture reached its highest point during 900 to 1100 C.E. The climate had more rainfall at that time, and the people carefully irrigated and managed the water supply. The Anasazi structures were multistoried dwellings built of stone. Timber was used for rooftops and ceilings, and a whitewash covered the exterior of their dwellings. The doorways and windows were narrow slits. The Anasazi frequently located their homes inside cliffs or in otherwise inaccessible locations, and sometimes ladders had to be climbed in order to get into the buildings, possibly for defensive purposes. The Anasazi also built ball courts and kivas. Kivas are keyhole-shaped underground structures where the Anasazi practiced religious ceremonies. Chaco Canyon, which had a population of ten thousand people or more, had an extensive roadway and irrigation system. Other Anasazi settlements are scattered throughout Arizona, New Mexico, and Colorado.

The Indians of the Southwest after the Anasazi, especially the Pueblo Indians, incorporated many of the features of Anasazi architecture into their structures, and it, in turn, has influenced what has come to be known as Southwest-style architecture. Indian architecture is alive and well today, and there are buildings being constructed that have a great deal of influence from some of the ancient Indian architecture, as well as new styles being developed by present-day Indian architects.

— J. D. Berry

SEE ALSO:

Anasazi; Aztec; Cahokia; Central America, Indigenous People of; Central and South Andean Culture Area; Chaco Canyon; Inca; Kiva; Maya; Mesa Verde; Mexico, Indigenous Peoples of; Mixtec; Mound Builders; Olmec; Pueblo; Toltec.

SUGGESTED READINGS:

Josephy, Alvin M. *The Indian Heritage of America*. Rev. ed. Boston: Houghton Mifflin, 1991.

Nabokov, Peter, and Robert Easton. *Native American Architecture*. New York: Oxford University Press, 1989.

Swanson, Earl, et. al. *The Ancient Americas*. New York: Peter Bedrick Books, 1989.

Weatherford, Jack. *Native Roots*. New York: Crown, 1991.

ARIKARA

The Arikara, or Ricaree, are a Native American tribe of the Caddoan language group. Today, most of the Arikaras live on the Fort Berthold Reservation in North Dakota.

The oral history of the Arikaras tells of a time when the tribe was part of the Pawnee Nation. Sacred items in the Arikara medicine bundles also seem to support this connection. Between 1450 and 1750, the Arikaras moved north to the Great Plains and formed their own tribe. Although they adopted customs from tribes they met along the way, they kept much of their Pawnee language. By the late 1700s, the Arikaras had three thousand to four thousand tribal members.

The life of the Arikaras was typical of Native tribes living on the Great Plains before the arrival of the horse. The prairie country and its rivers were excellent for hunting and fishing; the soil allowed the growing of limited crops. While the men hunted and fished, the women farmed. Each spring, the women used hoes made from the shoulder blades of animals and rakes made of river reeds to prepare

the soil and plant seeds of corn, squash, pumpkin, and beans on land the size of about 1 acre (0.4 hectare). At harvesttime, the crops to be stored for winter were boiled, dried, and then kept in cellars within the houses. The women also collected berries to supplement the tribe's diet of grains, beans, and meat.

During the growing and harvesting season, the Arikaras lived in earth lodges that looked like small mounds and formed a village. Each lodge was built around four posts, with twigs and mud making up the walls and roof. The floor was dug deep into the ground so people could stand upright. A hole for smoke and a hole for the door were the only openings in the lodge. To keep wind and rain from their lodges, the Arikaras built long tunnels to the door holes, which they closed with wooden doors, and dug trenches around the outside.

Villages also had larger medicine lodges for healing the sick and for performing sacred ceremonies during planting and harvesting times. Originally, twelve sacred medicine bundles were important for these ceremonies. Today, only a few of them are

Several Mandan and Arikara Indians gather for a group photograph in 1874. By the mid-1800s, epidemic diseases and common enemies had compelled the Arikaras to form alliances with the Mandan and Hidatsa peoples.

left. In winter, the Arikaras followed the buffalo. Their meat served as food; their hides and bones were used for clothing, tools, and cooking utensils. During the winter hunt, lodges of animal skins made moving easier.

The Arikaras were known as peace loving rather than as great hunters or warriors and most often served as traders between their neighbors. With the Sioux, they traded for buffalo skins and meat, which, in turn, they exchanged for guns and horses with the European-Americans. They also traded their crops with the American Fur Company for tools, combs, beads, ammunition, and tobacco.

In 1823, trouble between the Arikaras and Euro-American traders led to the first fight of the U.S. Army with a Plains Indian tribe. Later, during the Plains Indian Wars, the Arikaras fought as scouts on the side of the United States against the Arikaras' traditional enemies, the Sioux. During the nineteenth century, wars with the Cheyennes and Sioux reduced their numbers, and, in 1837, a severe smallpox epidemic killed over 50 percent of the tribe. To keep alive as a group, the Arikaras joined with the friendly Mandans and Hidatsas, who had also lost many lives to the disease, and formed the Three Affiliated Tribes.

After the Plains Wars, missionaries built churches and schools among the Three Affiliated Tribes who had been moved to the Fort Berthold Reservation in North Dakota. In 1970, there were only 700 Arikaras left, but their numbers are increasing: their count was up to 1,583 during the 1990 U.S. Census.

SEE ALSO:
Buffalo; Caddo; Cheyenne; Hidatsa; Indian Medicines; Mandan; Missions for Indians, Christian; North Dakota; Pawnee; Siouan Nations.

ARIZONA

Arizona became a U.S. state in 1912. The name *Arizona* most likely comes from one of two Indian names: Ari-son, meaning "small spring" or Aleh-zone, meaning "young spring."

Paleo-Indian sites indicate that Native American people were in Arizona by 10,000 B.C.E. Many Native cultures flourished in Arizona in older times. These cultures included the Hohokam in southern Arizona, who built extensive canals; the Anasazi in northern Arizona; the Mogollon in the middle of the state; the Cochise in southern Arizona; and the Patayon in the western part of the state. All of these cultures mysteriously disappeared in about 1450 C.E., although other tribes probably contain elements of these former cultures.

In 1539, the first European contact occurred in Arizona, when Marcos de Niza claimed Arizona for Spain. In 1540, Francisco Vásquez de Coronado explored Arizona while searching for Cíbola, the famed "Seven Cities of Gold." The Spanish occupied Arizona and built several military outposts, or *presidios*, and missions. There was a good deal of warfare between Arizona Indians and the Spanish. In 1680, the Hopi people took part in the Pueblo Revolt that forced the Spanish out of New Mexico and Arizona for several years. In southern Arizona, Apache attacks were so constant and forceful that most Spanish settlements were abandoned by 1835.

In the early part of the nineteenth century, Arizona experienced a new invasion as Anglo-American settlers, ranchers, miners, and explorers began to enter the area. Kit Carson led a campaign against the Navajos in 1863 that ended their resistance. Several bands of Apaches, under famous leaders such as Mangas Colorados, Cochise, and Geronimo continued to fight to maintain their way of life. In 1886, Apache resistance ended when Geronimo surrendered to General Nelson Miles.

Arizona currently contains twenty-three reservations. Some of these reservations extend into other states, and some are very large. The Navajo Reservation, for example, is the size of the New England region.

The 1990 U.S. Census lists 203,527 Native Americans as Arizona residents, placing Arizona third among U.S. states in Native American population.

SEE ALSO:
Anasazi; Apache; Carson, Kit; Cochise; Coronado Expedition; De Niza, Marcos; Geronimo; Hopi; Pueblo Revolt of 1680; Spain.

ARKANSAS

Arkansas, which is bordered by Missouri, Tennessee, Mississippi, Louisiana, Texas, and Oklahoma, became the twenty-fifth U.S. state on June 15, 1836. In the early 1540s, a group of Spanish explorers led by Hernando de Soto passed through portions of present-day Arkansas. The chronicles of this expedition provide the first written records of Arkansas Indians. At that time, the Quapaws (from whom the name *Arkansas* is derived) lived at the mouth of the Arkansas River, the Osages lived north of the Arkansas River, and the Caddos lived in the southwest.

The Bluff Dweller Indians had been among the earliest inhabitants of what is now Arkansas. They lived in the northwestern part of the state before 1000 B.C.E. By 1000 C.E., Mound Builders had settled along the Mississippi River in Arkansas. One of their best-known mounds, largely because it was virtually destroyed by pot hunters in the 1930s, is Spiro Mound, which is actually just across the Arkansas border in present-day Oklahoma.

Some Cherokees moved into Arkansas from the east in the late 1700s. Sequoyah, who is noted for creating the Cherokee syllabary (alphabet), finished that massive project in Arkansas. The first school in Arkansas was Dwight Mission, established in 1822 near Russellville. Its students were Cherokee. Other Indian groups that lived in Arkansas before it became a state in 1836 included the Chickasaws, Choctaws, Creeks, Lenapes (Delawares), Kickapoos, Shawnees, and Tunicas.

The Cherokees, along with other Indian groups, were forced to move to Indian Territory (now Oklahoma) in the 1830s. In 1994, the United Keetoowah Band of Cherokee Indians in Oklahoma gained permission from the Bureau of Indian Affairs (BIA) to relocate in Arkansas. The band cited its need to gain a land base as the reason for the move. The United Keetoowah Band is now headquartered at Waldron, Arkansas, in the Ouachita Mountains.

The 1990 U.S. Census lists 12,773 Arkansas residents as American Indians. This ranks Arkansas thirty-third among all U.S. states in Native American population.

SEE ALSO:
Caddo; Cherokee; Cherokee Alphabet; Chickasaw; Choctaw; Creek; De Soto Expedition; Kickapoo; Lenape; Mound Builders; Oklahoma; Osage; Quapaw; Sequoyah.

ART AND DESIGN, NATIVE

Most Native American nations have no word for art, but art in many forms is an everyday expression in Native culture. The indigenous people of the Americas have strong spiritual beliefs and familial ties that were expressed artistically with natural materials prior to European contact. After European contact, new materials, such as beads, were introduced to both cultures, giving Native artists greater freedom to express their culture.

The earliest art forms and designs were for human adornment, including tattooing, ochre painting, and shell, bone, and stone jewelry. Native beliefs hold that everything in nature is alive and has a spirit, and decorating even simple objects like tools became a way of honoring gifts from the natural world that were bestowed upon the people. Thus, the earliest designs were nature related, even though some of them may seem abstract. Many designs represent mythological concepts, deities, spirits, or universal life forces. These designs and their daily use reinforced community beliefs and established tribal pride.

From region to region, and depending on the environment, American Indian people had different ways of expressing themselves artistically. The people of the Southwest, for example, developed angular designs that are reminiscent of such features of the land as rock formations, mesas, and canyons. The people of the Northeast, which was heavily forested and interlaced with rivers and lakes, developed patterns and designs that are more curvilinear or floral in nature to represent their worldview. Thus, to say something is simply an "Indian design" ignores or negates its specific regional origin or the tribal symbolism related to it. Inasmuch as the nations of the Northwest Coast are vastly different in belief from the Southeast nations, the stereotyping of American Indian art does not do it justice.

There are thousands of designs among hundreds of Native nations. Often designs overlap regionally, and some tribes borrow from each other or are

This clay tableta by Santa Clara Pueblo artist Nora Naranjo-Morse combines traditional shapes and designs with a lighter, contemporary touch.

designs with her. Much more overlapping of designs and creative styles occurred than is generally acknowledged, especially with the relocation of thousands of Native people to reservations where they lived in contact with other tribes. Evidence of this may be found in Oklahoma, where members of the Seneca Nations of New York, the Cheyenne Nation of Wyoming, the Omaha Nation of Nebraska, and Potawatomi, Sauk, and Fox people from the Great Lakes and numerous other tribes have created arts and designs that were vastly different from each other.

In addition, very often Native designs "belonged" to a particular family or clan, and honor and custom dictated that these designs were not used without permission of the owners. This holds true among beadworkers, quillworkers, potters, and totem pole carvers; it is a fairly universal concept among Native

influenced by other factors. For example, a piece of beadwork purported to be Cheyenne but with only traces of Cheyenne elements may actually have been made by an Arapaho woman who married into the Cheyenne Nation and brought her own

people. The reason for this is that some designs may have symbolism that is sacred or religious to the family or clan.

Often designs were merely decorative and pleasing and had no symbolism except on a personal level. Other examples may be ancient petroglyphs or rock art, some of which was spiritual to honor the animals and some of which was simply decorative. Caution should be taken not to assume that all designs are symbolic or sacred even though they may be suggestive of natural phenomena or spiritual beliefs. An example of this would be buffalo track patterns on moccasin tops or the thunderbird motif that is fairly universal among Native nations.

Among the tribes, many designs were used in many mediums. Mohawk cutout silverwork designs can also be found within the beadwork. Similarly, Crow beadwork designs and Crow painted parfleche have much in common. Additionally, Pueblo weaving and yarn embroidery resembles many painted pottery designs. A thorough understanding of one particular art form among a nation will help identify other art forms from that nation.

— J. Monture

SEE ALSO:
Baskets; Beadwork and Beadworkers; Dance, American Indian; Fancy Dance and Fancy Shawl Dance; Feathers and Featherwork; Institute of American Indian Arts; Jewelry, Native American; Kachina; Moccasins; Parfleche; Quillwork and Quillworkers; Regalia; Rock Art; Silversmithing, Navajo.

SUGGESTED READINGS:

Abbott, Lawrence. *I Stand in the Center of the Good.* Lincoln: University of Nebraska Press, 1994.

Archuleta, Margaret, and Rennard Strickland. *Shared Visions: Native American Painters and Sculptors in the Twentieth Century.* New York: The New Press, 1991.

Ashabranner, Brent. *To Live in Two Worlds.* New York: Dodd, Mead and Company, 1984.

Penney, David W., and George C. Longfish. *Native American Art.* Hugh Lauter Levin Associates, Inc., 1994.

These traditional Peruvian dolls are handmade out of fragments of original cloth dating from before the Spanish conquest in the sixteenth century. They were once used as grave offerings.

ARTISTS, AMERICAN INDIAN

Visual arts are an important part of every American Indian society, from the totem poles and ceremonial masks of the Northwest Coast cultures to

San Ildefonso, New Mexico, Pueblo potter Maria Montoya Martinez with one of her creations.

Santa Clara, New Mexico, Pueblo artist Nora Naranjo-Morse with one of her whimsical sculptures.

the pottery and baskets of the Southwestern tribes. Traditionally, Native art objects served their respective communities because they were useful. In the twentieth century, however, Native artists, craftspeople, and artisans began to create their art for art lovers throughout the world. Here are profiles of a few of the many outstanding Native artists who have contributed or are contributing to their own cultures and to the world at large. Their work offers a sampling of the larger groupings of themes, techniques, and media that are explored in more detail in the encyclopedia entries listed at the end of this article.

T. C. Cannon, who lived from 1946 to 1978, was of Caddo, Choctaw, Kiowa, and European descent. He studied art at the Institute of American Indian Arts (IAIA) in Santa Fe, New Mexico, and at the San Francisco Art Institute. Many of his paintings are self-portraits that portray him as an artist, a traditionally dressed Indian, a cowboy, and an art collector. One of his paintings, titled *Collector #5*, symbolizes Cannon as both a contemporary artist who draws inspiration from his Native heritage and from his knowledge of and passion for European art. In the painting, a traditionally dressed Indian man sits in a wicker chair on top of a Navajo rug, while on the wall behind him hangs a van Gogh painting.

Maria Montoya Martinez lived from 1884 to 1980. A Pueblo potter, she paved the way for many of the other artists in her ancient village of San Ildefonso in New Mexico to gain economic security through the creation of distinctive and beautiful pottery. She learned the art of traditional Pueblo pottery making from her aunt. Later in her career, an archaeologist who had uncovered some fragments of an unknown type of shiny black pottery asked Maria and her husband, Julian Martinez, if they could reconstruct the pottery he had found. The couple researched and experimented and eventually discovered a method of firing the clay that reproduced the dark, glowing finish. This type of black pottery became their specialty; today the pots are easily recognized as San Ildefonso Blackware.

Pueblo artist Nora Naranjo-Morse, from Santa Clara, New Mexico, creates pottery using traditional methods but fuses it with her own distinct sense of irony and fun. One of her creations is a sculpture called *Pearlene Teaching Her Cousins Poker*. This sculpture depicts ritual clowns who are female rather

Chiricahua Apache sculptor and painter Allan Houser. Known primarily for his large-scale sculptures, Houser saw his work placed in museums throughout North America and in Europe.

than male, which is more typical. They are playing a game of poker, which they are learning from a book.

Jolene Rickard is a Tuscarora (Iroquois) artist and photographer from upper New York State. She uses photography, color Xerox, and collage in expressing her ideas on contemporary Native art. A photograph called *Self Portrait—Three Sisters* contains her image and two ears of corn. This signifies the Iroquois' traditionally held belief in their people's sacred relationship to corn. In fact, within many Indian nations, corn, beans, and squash are called *The Three Sisters*.

Oscar Howe, who lived from 1915 to 1983, is a well-known Yankton Sioux graphic artist. He was born in Joe Creek, South Dakota, on the Crow Creek Reservation. After graduating from Pierre Indian School in South Dakota, he studied painting at the U.S. Indian School in Santa Fe, New Mexico, and received further training in mural techniques at the Indian Art Center in Fort Sill, Oklahoma. Howe taught for many years in high schools

and later became a professor of fine arts at the University of South Dakota. Howe's paintings reflect poignant images of Indian culture in transition. He wished for his work to present the Sioux Indian's cultural way of life and offer the best things of Indian culture to the contemporary world.

Allan Houser, a Chiricahua Apache, was an internationally renowned sculptor and painter who lived from 1914 to 1994. Born in Oklahoma, he attended Santa Fe Indian School in New Mexico and later studied art at Utah State University. In the late 1940s, he was commissioned to create a half-ton (0.45-metric-ton) marble sculpture called *Comrade in Mourning*, which was a memorial to the Indian casualties of World War II. In 1949, his career as an artist was established when he was awarded a prestigious fellowship from the Guggenheim Foundation. He retired as head of the sculpture department of the Institute of American Indian Arts in 1975 and continued to exhibit his paintings and sculptures until his death in 1994.

Linda Lomahftewa is a Hopi-Choctaw painter whose art highlights the Plains Indians' traditional culture. She was born in 1947 in Phoenix, Arizona, and attended IAIA and the San Francisco Art Institute in 1971. She has held various teaching positions, including ones at the San Francisco Art Institute and the University of California. Her paintings have been displayed in over forty exhibitions, from New York City to Santa Fe, New Mexico. She is listed as one of many prominent figures of contemporary Native American Art in two editions of *Who's Who in American Indian Arts*.

Kevin Redstar, born in 1942 on the Crow Reservation in Lodge Grass, Montana, is of Crow and other northern Plains Indian heritage. He studied at IAIA and later at the San Francisco Art Institute, where he received a scholarship in 1965. While a first-year student there, he was awarded the governor's trophy and the Al and Helen Baker Award from the Scottsdale National Indian Arts Exhibition. In 1971, he held his first show at the Museum of the Plains Indian in Montana. His artwork draws mainly from the Plains Indian culture, especially Crow designs, "as a way to interpret a life force that goes beyond the one dimension of decorated objects." As an artist-in-residence at the Institute of American Indian Arts, he expanded his art to include serigraphs, lithography, and etchings. In 1977, he was selected as Artist of the Year by *Sante Fean* magazine.

Pablita Velarde is a Pueblo painter, born in 1918 in the Santa Clara Pueblo of New Mexico and educated at the Santa Fe Indian School. One of her most recognized works is a series of painted murals that depict the culture of the Rio Grande Pueblos. Her very original painting technique consists of grinding colored rocks and blending them to create a textured paint. One of her most famous paintings is *Old Father, the Story Teller;* she is also the author and illustrator of a book with the same title.

SEE ALSO:
Art and Design, Native; Baskets; Beadwork and Beadworkers; Feathers and Featherwork; Houser, Allan; Institute of American Indian Arts; Jewelry, Native American; Kachina; Martinez, Maria Montoya; Moccasins; Parfleche; Quillwork and Quillworkers; Regalia; Rock Art; Silversmithing, Navajo.

ASIA

Asia and Native America have been linked in the minds of many people for at least two reasons: first, when landing in the Bahamas, Christopher Columbus firmly believed that he had found the sea route to Asia; and second, most archaeologists hold that the original inhabitants of the Americas migrated here from Asia.

Europeans of the fifteenth century loved the silks from China and the spices from India. But the overland trade routes to these treasures were long and treacherous. By sailing west, navigators believed they could shorten the route and bring those goods back more quickly and safely. When Columbus saw land, he was—and stayed—convinced that he had reached the outer islands of the "Indies," the name Europeans then gave to all of Asia east of the Indus River. For him, it was therefore logical to call the people he encountered *Indios*.

Explorers after Columbus soon realized that he had reached a "New World," filled not with silks or spices but with the gold and silver that the Spanish desired even more. After the first Indians had been exhibited in Europe, scholars began to debate their state and origin: Who were they? Human beings or—since they were not mentioned in the Bible—creatures without souls? In 1537, Pope Paul III settled this issue by officially declaring that Indians belonged to the human race and could be Christianized. But this left another question wide open to speculation: Where did the Indians come from?

Early scholars tried to solve the puzzle of the Indians by consulting the sources they knew best: the Bible and classical writings. Biblical sources led scholars to argue on the one hand that Indians stemmed from the devil, and on the other, that they were the offspring of a separate Adam and Eve, created specifically by God for the "New World." The same sources supported the belief that Indians were descendants of Noah or members of the Lost Tribes of Israel. When studying classical texts, scholars argued that Indians migrated to the Americas from ancient lands—Polynesia, China, Greece, Spain, Egypt, Plato's lost continent (Atlantis), Carthage, or Troy.

Few of these stories are still believed today (although the *Book of Mormon* says that American Indians are descendants of the ancient Hebrews

Two Mongolian women of Kazakh descent wait to leave for their ethnic homeland in neighboring Kazakhstan. In 1992, when this photo was taken, Kazakhstan was a republic in now-former Soviet Central Asia. Most scholars feel that Asians and Native Americans may share a common ancestry, while others offer objections to this theory.

and are thus related to the Jews). And yet, the most widely held theory about the origins of Native Americans—that they migrated to the American continent from Asia—is also over four hundred years old; but today it is supported with archaeological findings. In 1590, a Spanish priest, José de Acosta, speculated that Indians must have crossed into the Americas on a land bridge that connected the old world to the new world.

Although Acosta did not know this then, Asia and America almost touch in the high north, separated only by the sixty-mile- (ninety-seven-kilometer-) wide Bering Strait. During the last Ice Age, when sea levels fell several times, this passage is said to have turned into a small continent, or subcontinent, ten times wider than the original strait. Archaeologists today speak of it as Beringia and believe that Stone Age Siberian hunters moved onto this landmass as they followed herds of woolly mammoth, bison, and reindeer. Although the climate must have been extremely harsh, scholars assume that these hunters could live in Beringia.

In order to explain the physical differences among American Indians and Inuit people, archaeologists assume that several migrations took place, during which these hunters moved into eastern Beringia, the Alaska of today. From there, they spread south into the entire continent.

Why do scholars consider Asia the homeland of Paleo-Indians (Indians of ancient times)? When, according to archaeologists, did the ancestors of today's Native Americans arrive in North America? There are several reasons why scholars believe that Paleo-Indians migrated here from Asia. One of these reasons is tied to physical, genetic, and linguistic characteristics: American Indians seem closer to Asian people than to any other group in the world; they and aboriginal Asian people show similar dental patterns. For example, they both have shovel-shaped incisors and a similar distribution of molar roots. There are also common blood group markers, and languages spoken on both sides of the Bering Strait are said to be related. Also, scholars find similarities in the use of symbols and rituals.

A Navajo sand painter. Some observers feel that similarities between Navajo and Tibetan sand paintings point to common cultural origins between Asians and American Indians.

For example, some people see connections between Tibetan and Navajo sand paintings. Like the Navajos, the Tibetan lamas also destroy their paintings when they are done.

One could argue—and some archaeologists (Jeffrey Goodman, for example) and lay people have done so—that these first two reasons are not convincing. Paleo-Indians could have originated in the Americas, migrated to Asia, and from there populated the rest of the world. But since the oldest remains of prehumans have been found in Africa, anthropologists claim that human beings evolved there. No such ancient fossils have been discovered in North, Central, or South America, and so most anthropologists feel that Native Amer-

icans must have arrived here after the development of what archaeologists call *homo sapiens sapiens*, modern human beings. Thus, one compelling argument against the theory of an America-to-Asia migration is lack of evidence.

The move of Paleo-Indians from Siberia (in Asia) into Alaska (in America), is also fairly well supported with archaeological findings on both sides of the Bering Strait. Controversial, however, is the date of their arrival. Because earth movements, weather, and water often relocate fossils, weapons, and tools, these objects are difficult to date accurately. Archaeologists are generally cautious, and most agree that the ancestors of Native Americans arrived from Asia relatively late, that is, between twelve thousand and fourteen thousand years ago. Still, there are also claims for migrations before this time, perhaps as early as twenty-five thousand to thirty-five thousand years ago.

The notion that Columbus found a new trade route to Asia was dispelled rather quickly, but the sixteenth-century hypothesis that Indians arrived in the Americas via a land bridge has lived on. In fact, it has been strengthened in our time through archaeological proof. The overwhelming majority of scholars believes that human beings originated in Africa, then dispersed through the so-called Old World, and finally reached the Americas after crossing the continent of Beringia. The connection with Asia is also supported by some Native American authors—Leslie Marmon Silko and Gerald Vizenor, for example—who evoke Asia in their writings. Another Native American writer, N. Scott Momaday, said in an interview that crossing the land bridge is "part of [his] racial memory."

Vine Deloria, Jr.'s controversial book *Red Earth, White Lies: Native Americans and the Myth of Scientific Fact*, challenges widely accepted scientific explanations about American Indians. He argues that Indians originated in the Americas and tries to disprove the Bering Strait theory.

A final but important thought: In addition to the view of various members of the scientific community, one must also consider the Native view when talking about homelands and origins. While archaeologists regard creation accounts as unscientific, many Native Americans have never questioned their beginnings. They still live the sacred stories, which tell members of a tribe where they came from. Myths of the Northwest talk of descending to this world through a hole in the sky; Southwestern stories, like those from the Navajo and the Pueblo Indians, describe a climb through successive worlds into the present one; the Cherokee and Cree know stories that speak of long migrations from west to east. As Alvin M. Josephy, Jr., writes in *500 Nations*, like the biblical story of creation in Genesis (the first book of the Jewish Scriptures and the Christian Bible), Native American origin myths have been cherished as "matters of faith and spiritual truth."

— H. Z. Weidner

SEE ALSO:
Alaska; *America and Americans*; Beringia; Cherokee; Columbus, Christopher; Creation Stories; Deloria, Vine, Jr.; India; Inuit; Jews; Momaday, N. Scott; Mormons; Navajo; Pueblo; Silko, Leslie Marmon; Vizenor, Gerald.

SUGGESTED READINGS:
Deloria, Vine, Jr. *Red Earth, White Lies: Native Americans and the Myth of Scientific Fact*. New York: Scribner, 1995.
Josephy, Alvin M., Jr. *500 Nations*. New York: Knopf, 1994.

ASSINIBOINE

Assiniboine is a name from French-Cree or French-Ojibwe (Chippewa) that means "People Who Cook with Stone." It was given to a portion of the Wazikute band of the Yanktonai Sioux who migrated north during the eighteenth century from present-day Minnesota to the St. Lawrence River. While living along the St. Lawrence River, the Assiniboines were visited by a Catholic priest, who tried to convert them to Christianity.

The Assiniboines migrated further west, stopping for a time in the area of Regina, Saskatchewan, Canada. They might have gone as far north as the Arctic Circle before settling along the banks of the Assiniboine and Saskatchewan Rivers, where they became allied with the Crees. They acquired trade goods, pots, and knives from the Hudson's Bay Company, which they took south to trade with the Mandans and Gros Ventres.

In 1780, a major smallpox epidemic destroyed about eight hundred Assiniboine families. By 1820, the Assiniboines had moved to northwestern Montana and northern North Dakota. In this new home, their old relatives, the Sioux, became their enemies, as did the Gros Ventres and the Arapahos. The Assiniboines remained allies with the Crees and also became allied with the Mandans.

Some Assiniboines, the Stoneys, moved back to Canada. They became involved with the Louis Riel rebellion against the Canadian government. When the rebellion failed, thirty Assiniboines were hanged, but the Stoneys remained in Canada nonetheless.

The Montana Assiniboines went west to the Fort Benton area, to Fort Assiniboine, south of Chinook. While at Fort Assiniboine, they rescued survivors from the Nez Perce leader Chief Joseph's battle with the U.S. Army in the nearby Bear Paw Mountains. They had been ordered to kill escaping Nez Perce but refused and pretended to bury them. Some Nez Perce were held in a stockade to prevent the Assiniboines from giving them any further help. Assiniboine women rescued Nez Perce children and later sent them home.

The Assiniboines signed the 1851 Fort Laramie Treaty, which recognized their right to hunt buffalo on their own buffalo range. They settled along the Milk River and in the Little Rocky Mountain area at the Fort Belknap agency. In 1878, the Gros Ventres settled nearby. When the United States government ordered the Fort Belknap agency closed and told the Assiniboines to move east to Fort Peck, only one band, Red Stone's clan, went to the fort. Descendants of that band still live at Fort Peck, which they share with the Sioux. A reservation at Fort Belknap was proposed by treaty in May 1888 and was formed in 1889. It consisted of 840,000 acres (340,200 hectares) of rolling prairie and mountains. Between eight hundred and eleven hundred Assiniboines settled there.

There has been very little written about the Assiniboines. They kept away from European-Americans as much as possible, and few writers who did encounter them saw much to record. The Assiniboines never really accepted the priests who came to try to convert them, and they kept their old religious traditions. Today, after years of opposing the traditional Sun Dance religion, members of the Catholic Church living among the Assiniboines now attend the Sun Dance.

Today, the Assiniboines and Gros Ventres share the Fort Belknap Reservation. Lodgepole, north of the Little Rocky Mountains, consists mainly of Assiniboines. Hays, across the mountains, is largely Gros Ventre. Settlement around the Fort Belknap agency in the northern part of the reservation is a mixture of both tribes. The northern edge of the reservation is a few miles (kilometers) from the Canadian border. Harlem, Montana, is located just off the reservation, across the Milk River from the agency.

— R. Gordon

SEE ALSO:

Arapaho; Chief Joseph; Gros Ventres; Hudson's Bay Company; Mandan; Montana; Nez Perce; North Dakota; Ojibwe; Riel, Louis; Saskatchewan; Siouan Nations; Smallpox.

Crispus Attucks, whose mixed African and Native ancestry and role in the American Revolution have made him a unique historical figure.

ATTUCKS, CRISPUS
(c. 1725–1770)

Son of a Black father and a Massachuset Indian mother, Crispus Attucks, also known as Small Deer, was the first casualty in the cause of the American Revolution. Attucks's father was an African slave in a Framingham, Massachusetts, household until about 1750, when he escaped and became a sailor. His mother lived in an Indian mission at Natick, Massachusetts.

The Boston Massacre took place on March 5, 1770, five years before the first sustained combat of the American Revolution at Lexington and Concord. Boston residents, who were upset with the Townshend Acts directing them to pay unwanted taxes, attacked a detachment of British troops in front of the city's customs house. The troops fired into the rioters (some accounts say that Attucks was their leader), killing Attucks first. Two others died on the spot of gunshot wounds, and two more died of their injuries later. In 1888, a monument to Attucks was erected on the Boston Common.

SEE ALSO:

American Revolution; Massachusetts.

AZTEC

The Aztec culture is an advanced North American civilization that reached its height in central Mexico in the sixteenth century. The name *Aztec* is derived from Aztlán, the semimythical location where Aztec legends say their culture originated. (*Aztlán* means "Place of the Herons," and from it is derived *Aztec*, meaning "People of the Heron Place.")

The Aztec people started as a small nomadic tribe that called themselves not Aztec but Mexica or Tenochca and were part of a collective tribal group called Chichimeca ("People of the Dog"). In the twelfth century, the Mexica nomads started migrating south and, over a period of several hundred years, eventually settled in what is today the valley of central Mexico, where they founded the town of Tenochtitlán. From this stronghold, the Aztecs sent armies to conquer large parts of Mexico and developed an advanced civilization. They built enormous cities, fought many wars, and created beautiful art and poetry—all without the use of metal tools, the wheel, beasts of burden, or alphabetic writing.

The funeral vase and cover depicted in this engraving are unmistakably Aztec in design and in the human face that adorns the side of the vase.

Expansion of the Aztec Empire

The Aztec Empire was made up of powerful independent city-states that often warred with each other for power and territory. Eventually, some of these city-states banded together to defeat the others, and, by 1431, Tenochtitlán became powerful enough to control the entire valley. This ruling alliance then turned outward in a massive program of military expansion that was in full force when the Spaniards arrived in 1519. Under the rulership of Moctezuma I (also known as Montezuma), the Aztecs expanded their empire from the Atlantic to the Pacific. At its height, a total of 489 cities paid tribute to the ruling alliance. These conquered cities provided food to feed the growing population of Tenochtitlán, as well as the luxury goods Aztec nobles and warriors could not find in central Mexico—goods such as gold, copper, tropical feathers, gemstones, rubber, jade, amber, jaguar skins, and chocolate. The conquering Aztec armies also took war captives, whom they brought back to Tenochtitlán for sacrifice to the gods.

These conquered cities strongly resented the harsh Aztec rule, and many were waiting for a chance to rebel. When Hernán Cortés arrived in 1519, they got their chance. Several Mexican cities willingly joined forces with his Spanish army, and with the help of these Indian allies, Cortés was able to conquer Tenochtitlán. The entire Aztec Empire crumbled shortly thereafter. However, in spite of the Spanish conquest and their introduction of Christian religion to Mexico, certain cultural and religious traditions from the Aztec heritage managed to survive.

ed monumental stone figures of gods and goddesses to decorate great temples, while others worked with gold and precious stones to create delicate mosaics and intricate jewelry. Other important artifacts include pottery, woven cloth, baskets, and feathered ornaments.

Trade was another important aspect of Aztec culture. A special class of merchants devoted themselves to long-distance commerce outside the Aztec Empire, and their caravans traveled as far as the Yucatán Peninsula and Guatemala, where they exchanged goods with Mayan traders. These merchants were also often used as official envoys and spies.

The Aztec Way of Life

The state controlled every aspect of Aztec life, setting rules for everyday behavior as well as rules relating to a person's social position. Society was divided into classes of nobles and commoners, with a special class of merchants and artisans in between. Everyone, regardless of class, was expected to live an "exemplary life," which stressed obedience, honesty, modesty, energy, and the fulfillment of whatever duties and responsibilities came with the person's class. A person could improve his or her social status by learning a skill or, for men, showing courage in battle.

An Aztec man was expected to be the provider for and protector of his family and, whether commoner or noble, was supposed to be eager to go to war and fearless on the battlefield. High-ranking nobles were allowed to have more than one wife. Women were expected to be devoted wives and mothers and to be especially skilled at weaving cloth and preparing food. Aztec children were expected to be respectful, obedient, and humble. While they received a strong moral and practical education within the home, children between the ages of twelve and fifteen were also required to attend a school, where they learned to sing, dance, and play musical instruments for important religious ceremonies. At fifteen, boys of the noble class went on to a more formal school, where they studied with priests to learn history, writing, calendars, martial arts, and the law.

An Aztec drummer performs in regalia with his dance group in Mexico City. Mexico's huge capital city is built over the original Aztec capital, Tenochtitlán.

Aztec Culture

At the height of the Aztec Empire, urban communities consisted of groups of families who jointly owned large pieces of cultivated land. These family groups were required to give part of their crop yield to the state each year as a kind of tax. Corn (or maize) was important, but crops such as wheat and barley were unknown until the Spanish introduced them. Although they had no horses or other beasts of burden, the Aztecs were efficient farmers who used effective irrigation, terracing, and fertilizing techniques.

Aztec craftsmen used copper and bronze tools, but not iron. Strangely, they knew about the wheel but never applied the concept to wheeled vehicles or machines with rotary parts. It was only used for children's pull-along toys.

The Aztecs also lacked glass and gunpowder, but this did not stop them from creating great works of art and magnificent buildings. Aztec art was both powerful and delicate. Some sculptors creat-

Games were played both for recreation and as part of religious rituals. A popular ball game was tlachtli, in which the players struck a small rubber ball with their hips or thighs, trying to knock it across a special court.

Aztec Spirituality

The Aztecs worshiped many gods who, they believed, demanded many offerings and sacrifices. Each god was connected with some aspect of the universe, such as rain and fertility, or served as a special protector of specific rulers, city-states, or craft groups. Because drought was a constant threat in most parts of central Mexico, farmers worshiped Tlaloc, the rain god. Another important god was Quetzalcoatl (also known as the feathered serpent), patron of arts and crafts and the god of self-sacrifice. But above all, the Aztecs considered themselves the chosen people of Huitzilopochtli, the sun and war god, in whose name they were destined to conquer all rival nations.

Although some of the Aztecs' public religious ceremonies evidently involved human sacrifice, the extent and nature of sacrifice has been a subject of sensationalist imagery and debate. While it is commonly understood that the Aztecs sacrificed enemy captives, the practice of human sacrifice in Aztec society may not have been as extensive or wanton as some popular views have held it to be. More important, the Aztecs are thought to have believed that they were responsible for maintaining the universe by continually offering their gods human blood, and there were ways of accomplishing this that fell considerably short of sacrificing living human beings. For example, priests, and sometimes the whole population, offered their own blood by piercing parts of their body with maguey thorns.

Many religious rituals took place in individual households, where a holy man might be called in to diagnose an illness or predict the outcome of a particular event. People also believed that certain omens (like a weasel crossing one's path or lightning striking a temple) could reveal important clues about the future.

The Aztecs developed a remarkably accurate ritual calendar of 365-day years, each divided into 18 months. Each day of the Aztec calendar marked a different festival, complete with music, dancing, and processions. They believed that every 52 years, the universe was on the brink of ending, but if they prayed and fasted and performed all the proper rituals, it would renew itself and a new life cycle would begin.

After the Fall

The Aztec Empire effectively ended when its leaders surrendered to Cortés in 1521. Soon after the conquest, Spanish friars arrived in Mexico to convert the Aztecs to Christianity and thereby supposedly save their souls. The religious training the friars offered did not have the desired effect. The Aztecs simply accepted the Christian god as just another of the many gods they already worshiped. The monastery schools provided Native children with more than religious training, however, and many were taught to read and write.

But the defeated Aztecs did not welcome or willingly accept the changes imposed upon them by the Spanish. Thousands of Aztec decendants still live in Mexico today, and while many speak Spanish, purchase prepared food in stores, and wear store-bought clothing, they still continue to practice many of the customs of their ancient culture. Many Aztec artisans still produce the traditional intricately designed pottery and woven cloth, still prepare meals the old way, and still maintain their language and spiritual beliefs.

— P. Press

SEE ALSO:

Architecture, Indian; Chichimec; Cortés, Hernán; Maya; Mexico, Indigenous Peoples of; Moctezuma; Spain.

SUGGESTED READINGS:

Bachelis, Faren. *The Central Americans*. New York: Chelsea House Publishers, 1990.

Berdan, Frances F. *The Aztecs*. New York: Chelsea House Publishers, 1989.

Stephen, David. *Central America's Indians*. London: Minority Rights Group, Ltd., 1984.

Stuart, George E. *Ancient Mexico: Aztec, Mixtec, and Maya Landscapes*. New Brunswick, NJ: Rutgers University Press, 1992.

Von Hagen, Victor Wolfgang. *The Ancient Sun Kingdoms of the Americas: Aztec, Maya, Inca*. Cleveland: World Publishing Co., 1961.

AZTLÁN

See Aztec.

BACONE COLLEGE

Bacone College is the oldest continuing school in what is now the state of Oklahoma. The American Baptist Home Mission Society founded the school on Christian principles in the Cherokee Nation in 1880. Originally located in Tahlequah, Indian Territory (present-day Oklahoma), the school was soon moved. It is named after its first teacher, professor Almon C. Bacone, a missionary. Working alone, he began the school for American Indian students and started teaching in Tahlequah.

At first, the school had only three students enrolled, but it grew quickly. After the first year, it had fifty-six students and three teachers, and a search was begun for a new and larger location. The Creek Nation Tribal Council was asked for a 160-acre (64-hectare) building site in Muskogee, known at that time as the Indian Capital of the World. The Creek Nation granted the request, and the school, then known as Indian University, was relocated in 1885 to Muskogee, Indian Territory. Classes were originally taught from first grade through four years of college.

In 1910, after Oklahoma was admitted to statehood, the school was renamed Bacone College after its founder and first president. The college continues today with many American Indian students, but all students are welcome. The original building in Tahlequah, Oklahoma, was recently restored and is now the tribal center for Northeastern Oklahoma State University.

See also:
Oklahoma.

BADLANDS NATIONAL MONUMENT

Through the Ecocene and Oligocene epochs between thirty-seven and twenty-three million years ago, rain, wind, and frost carved steep canyons, sharp ridges, gullies, spires, and knobs out of the prairie in the Badlands area of western South Dakota. Volcanic ash blown from the west formed the whitish layer that today characterizes the upper portions of the Badlands formations.

As the climate became warmer and drier, the forests and swamplands and their animals changed. Today, annual precipitation is only sixteen inches (about forty centimeters) and sustains a surprising array of grasses and animals. But with the coming of immigrants from the east, many species became extinct.

During their annual migrations through what is now Nebraska and the Black Hills, the Lakota people often camped along the White River, which flows along the boundaries of the Badlands. The Stronghold area became very important because, with only one way in or out, it offered safety and sanctuary from enemies. In 1890, the Lakotas in the Pine Ridge Reservation area who took up the Ghost Dance camped at the isolated Stronghold to escape both curiosity seekers and the interference by the agency superintendent. When Big Foot, the Miniconjou Sioux peace chief, led his people to Pine Ridge seeking safety in December 1890, they cut across a section of the northern Badlands. Many who fled Standing Rock after their chief Sitting Bull's assassination traveled with them. (Sitting Bull had recently been killed while in U.S. custody, having been arrested for his involvement with the Ghost Dance.) The U.S. Army stopped the group near Wounded Knee. There, on December 29, 1890, the army slaughtered between two and three hundred Native people, including the Big Foot band.

In 1929, Congress authorized the formation of the Badlands National Monument to preserve the scenery, protect fossils and wildlife, and conserve the mixed-grass prairie. During World War II, the United States took 265,000 acres (107,325 hectares) in the Badlands for an aerial gunnery range. People living in the area had only a few days to move out of their homes; most also lost their possessions and land. Although the government said it provided payments, no one actually received any compensation.

After the war, the United States offered 150,000 acres (60,750 hectares) of the range for repurchase

Striking natural rock formations and a variety of prairie grasses characterize the Badlands, a region that has played a key role in the history of Indian America and its relations with outside forces.

by the Indian owners at the U.S. purchase price plus 6 percent interest, which, in most cases, doubled the amount allegedly paid by the government. Few could raise the necessary funds. A Badlands area, rich in uranium and other minerals, cuts through almost the full width of the Pine Ridge Reservation. The Defense Department retained 43,163 acres (17,481 hectares) and placed 72,477 acres (29,353 hectares) under tribal administration with numerous restrictions on who could use it or live on it. Owners of the land retained the right to their property only for their lifetime; they could not pass the land on to their children.

In 1970, when the United States sought parts of the gunnery range and reservation land outside it to add to the Badlands National Monument, Leo Wilcox, an Oglala, led a protest at Sheep Mountain. Over the next four years, demonstrations consistently met the United States' periodic attempts to take land in this area. However, on June 26, 1975, with two supporters posing as tribal council land committee members, Tribal Chairman Dick Wilson signed over the Sheep Mountain area, high in uranium holdings, and other land to the Park Service in Washington, D.C. Coincidentally, on the same day in Oglala, FBI agents and local people, along with members of the American Indian Movement (AIM), engaged in a firefight, which was later documented in a movie entitled *Incident at Oglala*.

About half of the land taken, 133,300 acres (53,986 hectares), became part of the Badlands National Monument in 1976. Some of this land was eventually returned to the tribe. In 1978, the monument became the Badlands National Park. The tribe owns and the Park Service operates Cedar Pass Lodge at the northeastern entrance of the Badlands.

— C. Hamilton

SEE ALSO:

American Indian Movement; Big Foot; Black Hills; Ghost Dance Religion; *Incident at Oglala*; Pine Ridge Reservation, Conflict at; Siouan Nations; Sitting Bull; Wilson, Richard; Wounded Knee (1890).

BAHAMAS

The islands of the Bahamas form an enormous archipelago that extends from Grand Bahama Island, which lies about 60 miles (97 kilometers) off the coast of Florida, over 500 miles (805 kilometers) southeast to Great Inagua Island, which lies just 50 miles (81 kilometers) from the eastern tip of Cuba. The Bahamas are composed of about seven hundred islands and cays and over two thousand rocks. (A cay is a small, low island made up mostly of coral or sand.) The total land area has been estimated at over 5,000 square miles (13,000 square kilometers). The islands of the Bahamas are almost completely flat. The highest point is on Cat Island and measures only 400 feet (121 meters) above sea level. There are no rivers and streams, and while some of the land is fertile, it is also shallow. Only twenty-nine of the islands and cays of the Bahamas are inhabited, primarily because of the lack of fresh water and arable land. The Commonwealth of the Bahamas has been an independent nation since 1973, when it ended its colonial relationship with Britain.

Archaeological evidence reveals that the first inhabitants of the Bahamas were probably the Ciboney (Siboney), an early Caribbean culture that populated the Greater Antilles beginning in 500 B.C.E. They developed a prehistoric fishing-based culture, migrated down the Florida Peninsula and island-hopped through the Antilles. Much of this is archaeological speculation, however.

But it is known that in 1492, the Bahamas were inhabited by the Lucayans, a group of Arawak-speaking Indians who practiced a culture referred to as Tainan. These people migrated

The Bahamas are believed to have been home to indigenous people from both the Caribbean and mainland regions around the Gulf of Mexico. With the coming of European colonizers, Native cultures shrank in size and influence. Today, most Bahamians, like the Junkanoo dancers and musicians of Nassau shown here, are descended from African slaves.

through the Antilles, under pressure from the more aggressive Caribs, pushing on or assimilating the Ciboney as they went. The Lucayans were a race of farmers and fishermen. Because of the sparsity of resources in the Bahamas, such goods as pottery and hardwoods had to be imported, and agricultural production was largely limited to manioc and cotton.

The Bahamas hold a distinctive place in the history of the Americas. On October 12, 1492, Christopher Columbus made landfall at Long Bay, San Salvador Island, in the Bahamas. For the first time—in recorded history, at least—European culture made contact with the Native cultures of the Western Hemisphere. The Spanish found the inhabitants to be gentle and generous and, as seemed destined to become the case repeatedly, repaid the Native people's generosity with European contempt and treachery. Seven of the Lucayans who met the Spanish were forced to accompany Columbus on his onward voyage.

Once Columbus and his crew happened upon the island of Hispaniola (present-day Haiti and Dominican Republic), the Spanish had little use for the Bahamas. It was not until the Native populations of Hispaniola and Cuba were largely decimated by disease and overwork that the Spanish again looked to the Bahamas for the one resource that they could supply—slave labor. The process of moving the Native people from the Bahamas to Hispaniola began in earnest in 1509. For the Lucayans, overt resistance to the Spanish was impossible, as was flight. They followed their leader to Hispaniola.

In the relative isolation of the Bahamas, the Lucayans had been able to avoid the ravages of European diseases, but on the more densely populated Hispaniola, they succumbed quickly to epidemics of typhoid, malaria, smallpox, and pneumonia. By 1525, the Lucayans had virtually ceased to exist as a cultural force. The Bahamas themselves would remain obscure—and mostly unsettled—until English interest in the seventeenth century.

SEE ALSO:
Arawak; Caribbean, Indigenous Cultures of; Columbian Exchange; Columbus, Christopher; Cuba; Hispaniola; Taino.

BANKS, DENNIS (1932–)

Dennis Banks (Nowacumig) is a founding member of the American Indian Movement (AIM) and has become one of AIM's best-known leaders. Banks is an Ojibwe (Anishinabe or Chippewa) from Leech Lake, Minnesota. He was born in 1932 and taken from his family at age five to spend fourteen years in Bureau of Indian Affairs boarding schools. The boarding schools were located in North and South Dakota and in Minnesota.

In 1953, Banks joined the air force and spent three years in Japan. From that time until he joined forces with Clyde Bellecourt and other founders of AIM in 1968, he bounced around from the reservations to St. Paul and Minneapolis, Minnesota. Banks is considered eloquent and charismatic, with an instinct for inflammatory statements. His name and that of fellow AIM member Russell Means soon became synonymous with the AIM cause.

AIM is an organization founded in Minneapolis to fight for Native American rights. Banks told other AIM chapter leaders that in order for the Indian rights movement to be taken seriously, the AIM people had to get serious. In 1971, when the Trail of Broken Treaties was being organized, Banks was sent to San Francisco to get a caravan of people together. The caravan was to meet with numerous other AIM chapters at the Bureau of Indian Affairs (BIA) building in Washington, D.C., to air grievances regarding American Indian rights and needs to the federal government. After arriving at the capital, an armed BIA security guard tried to expel the group from the BIA building, and the group resisted. This event led to AIM occupying the building for a week, until the government agreed to consider the twenty demands outlined in the Natives' position paper.

Banks became AIM's field coordinator and met with a group at Custer, South Dakota, to demonstrate support for upgrading the charges to first-degree murder against a non-Native man who had stabbed a twenty-year-old Indian man to death. The event erupted in a riot after the mother of the dead man tried to enter Custer Courthouse and was shoved and beaten. Banks was accused of riot and assault but later received amnesty.

Traditional people of the Pine Ridge Reservation then asked for AIM's assistance with problems

American Indian Movement leader Dennis Banks, as photographed during the 1973 occupation of Wounded Knee, Pine Ridge, South Dakota.

Courthouse incident and fled to Canada. When he was arrested after coming back to South Dakota, his bail was set at $135,000. The trial against Banks, along with Russell Means, lasted eight and one-half months. The men were represented by the Wounded Knee Legal Defense/Offense Committee.

Between 1976 and 1983, Banks attended the University of California, Davis, and received an associate of arts degree. He also taught at D–Q University (named after Deganawidah and Quetzacoatl, two historic leaders representing Native traditions of northeastern North America and Central Mexico), where he became the first Native university chancellor.

Banks helped organized the Longest Walk, from Alcatraz to Washington, D.C., in 1978. The walk was to protest new anti-Indian legislation and the mass removal of Navajo people from the Big Mountain region in Arizona. The walk also staged a demonstration for Leonard Peltier (then convicted under suspicious circumstances of the murder of two federal agents on the Pine Ridge Reservation) and other political prisoners. Banks then organized a tribunal to consider evidence of U.S. human rights violations against indigenous populations.

they were having with their more assimilated tribal council, which was supported by the federal government. Banks assisted in the occupation of Wounded Knee on the Pine Ridge Reservation in 1973. The occupation of the small reservation town began in late February and lasted seventy-one days. A federal grand jury issued indictments against Banks, Clyde Bellecourt, Russell Means, Carter Camp, and Pedro Bissonnette dealing with the Wounded Knee occupation.

On August 5, 1973, Banks was elected as national director of AIM during the national convention in Oklahoma. One month later, he was indicted on charges stemming from the Custer

Throughout this time, Banks continued to be plagued by legal troubles stemming from his activist efforts. He went underground in 1982 and was given asylum by the Onondaga Reservation in New York. While there, he organized the Great Jim Thorpe Run from New York City to Los Angeles. In September 1984, he surrendered to South Dakota in order to put the Custer Courthouse case and the assault conviction behind him. He was sentenced to two concurrent terms of three years and served about a year and a half in prison.

Since then, Banks has organized a number of spiritual events, including a reburying ceremony for over twelve hundred Native grave sites disturbed by grave robbers in Kentucky and sacred runs across the United States and Japan. He has also written his autobiography, entitled *Sacred Soul*, and has had key roles in several Hollywood films about Native Americans. He also continues to play a leadership role in the American Indian Movement.

— S. S. Davis

SEE ALSO:

American Indian Movement; Bellecourt, Clyde and Vernon; Boarding Schools; Bureau of Indian Affairs; D-Q University; Longest Walk; Means, Russell; Peltier, Leonard; Pine Ridge Reservation, Conflict at; Trail of Broken Treaties; Wounded Knee, Confrontation at.

Native writer, editor, and educator José Barreiro, shown in 1995, has kept the public eye focused on numerous issues of concern to Native people throughout North America.

BARREIRO, JOSÉ (1948–)

Born in 1948 in Cuba and reared in the Taino culture there, José Barreiro (Taino-Cuban) emigrated to the United States at the age of twelve. He has edited the *Northeast Indian Quarterly* (renamed *Akwe:kon Journal* in 1992) under the auspices of the American Indian Program at Cornell University since the journal began publication in 1984. Barreiro also is the editor of Cornell's Akwe:kon Press. Under Barreiro's direction, Akwe:kon (which means "all of us" in Mohawk) combines missions of scholarship and community service. The journal, the press, and the Cornell American Indian Program have influenced a generation of scholars. Barreiro also contributed to the Cornell American Indian Program as it combined with other disciplines at Cornell to provide many of the early and critical studies of environmental pollution on Indian reservations, especially Akwesasne (St. Regis) in New York.

Akwe:kon Journal and the Cornell American Indian Program also have sponsored and published the proceedings of a number of important conferences, including "Cultural Encounter: The Iroquois Great Law of Peace and the United States Constitution," "Indian Corn of the Americas: A Gift to the World," and "Indigenous Economics: Toward a Natural World Order." In 1993, Barreiro published *The Indian Chronicles* (Arte Publico Press), a novelistic treatment of the first Spanish landfalls in the Americas as seen through Native American eyes. For the novel, Barreiro conducted original research in the archives of Spain.

SEE ALSO:

Akwesasne (St. Regis Reservation), Pollution of; Cuba; Taino.

Allie Reynolds, a Creek Indian who pitched himself a standout career with the Cleveland Indians and New York Yankees, as photographed in 1953.

Austin Ben Tincup, a Cherokee Native who played for the Philadelphia Phillies and Chicago Cubs before coaching for the Yankees, St. Louis Browns, and Phillies.

BASEBALL

Although the American Indian boarding schools funded by the U.S. government in the 1800s and early 1900s were harsh and demeaning, they did provide some Native students with the opportunity to participate in sports. The schools did not approve of traditional Indian sports, such as lacrosse and other competitive Indian ball games, but they did allow football, basketball, and baseball. Two schools that boasted particularly powerful baseball teams were the Carlisle Indian Industrial School in Carlisle, Pennsylvania, and the Haskell Institute in Lawrence, Kansas. These were industrial schools that offered vocational rather than college-level courses, but their students were nevertheless allowed to compete at the college level in football, basketball, track, swimming, and baseball.

Indian schools produced many talented athletes who went on to compete professionally, some of whom excelled in more than one sport. Some outstanding major league baseball players inducted into the American Indian Athletic Hall of Fame include Carlisle graduates Charles Bender, an Ojibwe (Chippewa) Hall of Fame pitcher for the Philadelphia Athletics from 1903 to 1917, and all-around Olympic athlete Jim Thorpe, a Sac and Potawatomi Indian who played baseball with the New York Giants from 1913 to 1919—and who excelled in ten other sports *besides* baseball. Outstanding Haskell graduates include Arapaho John Levi, who played with the Yankees in 1925, and Austin Ben Tincup, a Cherokee who played ball with the Philadelphia Phillies and Chicago Cubs in 1914 and 1915 and then went on to coach for the Yankees, Browns, and Phillies.

Another notable Indian baseball player was John Meyers of the Cahuilla Nation who played for the New York Giants (1908–1912) and the Brooklyn Dodgers (1916–1917). Meyers batted .358 in 1912. Creek Native Allie P. Reynolds pitched successfully for both the Cleveland Indians (1942–1946) and the New York Yankees (1947–1954). Reynolds had the best earned-run average in the American League in both 1952 and 1954, led the league in strikeouts and shutouts for two years, and was voted the United States Professional Athlete of the Year in 1951. Chickasaw Euel "Monk" Moore played professional ball with the Philadelphia Phillies (1934–1935), the New York Giants (1935), and then the Phillies again (1936–1937).

The first Native American to play in major league baseball was Lou Sockalexis, a Penobscot Indian from Maine who was educated and played baseball at Holy Cross and Notre Dame. In 1897, he was signed by the Naps, the Cleveland National League Club, and was an instant success as a right fielder. He had a strong throwing arm and was great at bat. At first, fans let out insulting war whoops when he came up to bat but stopped when they became aware of his skill and his pride in the game. Sockalexis had such a strong influence on both his team and the Cleveland fans that they renamed the team the Cleveland Indians.

Many traditional Indian games (like lacrosse) require the same kind of highly developed athletic abilities that make good baseball players, so it is only logical that Indians excel at the sport. Historically, games and sports have always played an important, often spiritual, part in Indian culture. Games were played to honor the dead, comfort those in mourning, influence the weather, heal the sick, and ensure fertility. The games benefited the tribe as a whole, and both players and spectators were enthusiastic participants.

There is one aspect of baseball, however, that many Native Americans continue to object to. They feel that Native American sports mascots and team names (like Chiefs, Redskins, and Red Raiders) reinforce insulting and racist Indian stereotypes. For the last twenty years, Indians and non-Indians alike have protested (often successfully) against Indian mascots and names being used by professional, college, and even high school sports teams. In 1972, for example, the Cleveland Indian Center filed a suit against the Cleveland Indians baseball team, objecting to the use of their "Chief Wahoo" mascot.

In 1991, American Indians protested outside the World Series games between the Atlanta Braves and the Minnesota Twins, not just for the name "Braves" but for the chopping gesture Atlanta fans used to imitate tomahawks in battle. In 1992, North American Indians helped form the National Coalition on Racism in Sports and the Media to continue the fight.

— P. Press

SEE ALSO:
American Indian Athletic Hall of Fame; Bender, Charles Albert; Carlisle Indian School; Haskell Indian Nations University; Sockalexis, Louis; Thorpe, Jim; Tomahawk Chop.

BASKET MAKER

Basket Maker is the term used by archaeologists for an early stage of development of Anasazi Culture in the Southwest. The Anasazis were the ancestors of the contemporary Pueblo peoples.

Before 1927, archaeologists divided Basket Maker Culture into two stages, Basket Maker and Modified Basket Maker. In 1927, at a famous gathering of the leading archaeologists of the Southwest known as the first Pecos Conference, archaeologists agreed upon a new division for discussing Basket Maker artifacts and cultural development. This arrangement divides Basket Maker Culture into three phases: Basket Maker I, for the long period of time before 700 B.C.E.; Basket Maker II, from about 700 B.C.E. to about 400 or 450 C.E.; and Basket Maker III, from about 450 B.C.E. to about 750 C.E. The new feature of this arrangement was the creation of the Basket Maker I category.

Archaeologists speculate that Basket Maker Culture began to develop when the nomadic Archaic Desert Culture people of the Southwest started to depend more on crops they raised themselves, rather than gathering the wild bounty of nature. As a result, they became more sedentary. This is a shadowy period of development that is estimated to have covered about three thousand years. Hardly any sites have been found for this Basket Maker I period. Excavations of the few that have been found indicate that the people used projectile points (such as arrowheads), stone grinding tools, hearths, and an elementary form of basketry using single strand, interlocking stitches. Caves and overhanging ledges were used for shelter. However, not enough sites from this period have been found for archaeologists to agree about its cultural features. Although more evidence is needed, Basket Maker I was given a place in the classification system because archaeologists believe that eventually enough sites will be found to provide an adequate study.

During the Basket Maker II period, a period that is sometimes still referred to simply as Basket Maker, most of the people continued living in natural shelters provided by overhanging ledges and caves. Some of them, though, began constructing houses of a distinct type, called pit houses. These were forerunners of the kiva. The kiva would later be used in Anasazi Culture as a separate, underground structure for religious and clan purposes; this happened once stone masonry apartments began to be constructed for housing. One distinguishing feature of Basket Maker II, and the one that originally gave the culture the name by which it is now known, is the large quantity of baskets found at these sites. Other kinds of woven artifacts are also much in evidence. These include bags, robes, aprons, and sandals. The people cultivated maize and squash to supplement the gathering of wild seeds. Darts were used for hunting, as were atlatls, or spear throwers.

Another distinguishing feature of the Basket Maker II phase, which is still sometimes referred to as Modified Basket Maker, is the widespread use of pottery. The people learned how to domesticate turkeys, and the bow and arrow replaced the atlatl and dart. The people relied increasingly on agriculture, as indicated by the construction of pit house villages. Some of these villages contain early examples of what would later become the great kivas, or very large ceremonial structures. Crops included maize, beans, and squash, although the people still continued to harvest wild plant foods, including acorns, sunflower seeds, juniper berries, piñon nuts, pigweed, yucca fruit, and rice grass. Trade items such as marine shells, turquoise pendants, and distinctive pottery designs found their way to this area from as far away as the Pacific Coast and northern Mexico.

The eighth century was a transition period. During this time Basket Maker Culture gradually took on the characteristics that are now recognized as those of Anasazi Culture. In time, Anasazi Culture gradually passed through a number of stages. Eventually, it became transformed into the culture of the contemporary Pueblo peoples of the Southwest. By classifying the various stages of cultural change into periods based on the distinguishing features of each era, archaeologists are able to show a continuous linking of one culture to another,

stretching far back into the distant past. The Pueblo peoples of the Southwest are indeed an ancient people upon the earth.

— D. L. Birchfield

SEE ALSO:
Anasazi; Baskets; Kiva; Pueblo.

BASKETS

The earliest handcrafted containers used for carrying and storing goods in North America were Native American baskets. Archaeologists have discovered basketry fragments at sites in the Great Plains and Southwest culture areas that predate the appearance of Europeans on the continent. The Anasazis, ancestors of the Pueblo people, were early basket makers, who created decorated bowls, jars, and burden baskets, using the same techniques basket makers use today. Some of these early baskets date back more than eight thousand years, significant evidence of the enduring history of this craft.

In historic times, a wide variety of Indian baskets were created to serve everyday needs. Baskets were used in all stages of life, from baby cradles to ritual baskets and funeral jars for the dead. In everyday life, basketry was used for clothing such as hats and for water bottles. Baskets were used in preparing food, from gathering and storing foodstuffs to processing work, such as refining grains with seed beaters and winnowing trays. Some tribes used baskets for cooking. Rather than place cooking baskets directly into the fire, rocks were heated and added to the food.

Basketry work included not only the actual crafting of the baskets but also gathering and preparing materials. Growing and harvesting as well as preparation were year-round activities. In some Native cultures, gathering materials was performed as a ritual with great reverence to the source. Most often, basketry work was performed by women, however, in some cultures, the men also crafted baskets. For example, Pomo Indian men made simple objects such as fish traps and cradles.

Basket makers exhibited a great deal of ingenuity in collecting materials for their work. A wide variety of vegetable materials were used,

A Papago woman displays her basketry work in Covered Wells, Arizona.

including all kinds of grasses and roots, hemp, reeds, willow, bark, ferns, or any other useful plant material available in the region. Birch bark and hardwood splints were popular in the Northeast, while Southwest tribes used more grasslike materials. The animal kingdom also provided a variety of basketry materials. Different tribes used feathers, quills, teeth, moose hair, and rawhide in their baskets. Arctic-area people sometimes used baleen, a material harvested from the upper jaws of whales, in their basket construction.

The form and shape of the basket depended on its purpose. The Southwest and Great Basin tribes manufactured large cone-shaped carrying baskets for transporting items or collecting food. The Pacific Northwest Indians created cylindrical or dome-shaped hats with flaring rims that were waterproof and protected the wearer from rain. Mohegan basketry work included twined bags used for transporting and storing corn. The Klikitat Indians of the Cascades-Plateau region made tall and narrow

cylindrical baskets used for packing on horses. Size varied from small trinket baskets made by northern California tribes to large 4-foot-(122-centimeter-) high storage jars that took Southwest basket weavers as long as two years to make.

There were also baskets with less practical uses. Indians of the Plains made coiled gambling baskets to use for dice games. California tribes also wove gambling trays. Special basketry work was performed for ceremonial objects. The Dakota Sioux had a special ritual for weaving and assembling war bundles that carried sacred objects and protected the owner from harm. Southern California desert Indians created intricately decorated bottleneck-style baskets to hold rattlesnakes for the World Renewal Ceremony. Yurok Indians in Northern California wove ceremonial "purses" for use in the Jump Dance ceremony.

Basket-weaving techniques are divided into a couple of basic methods. Most basketry is either woven or sewn. Woven baskets are the sturdiest

A Hopi basket colored with plant dyes.

and are formed by any number of variations of plaiting and twining. Both plaiting and twining are methods of interweaving weft, the more flexible fibers that run horizontally, with the warp, the stiffer fibers that run lengthwise. Southeast basketry is distinguished by its twill-plaited style and the use of glossy cane materials. The other basket-making technique, coiling, is sewn. With this method, a long coil of stiff material or bundle of materials is held in shape by stitching. This method is popular with Indians in the Southwest.

Baskets had practical value but were also objects of beauty. Decorative patterns and the shape of the basket itself had ritual or cultural significance. Most woven designs are geometric because of the way the materials are put together and often follow a simple repeating pattern. Animal shapes and trib-al symbols also decorate baskets. A large range of color could be added by dyeing materials, using various plant sources. Southeast basketry is known for its highly developed use of color. Color could also be added with decorative feathers, quills, shells, and, in the Arctic regions, carved ivory.

In contemporary life, basket making is still a greatly valued skill. However, few baskets are produced for practical use. Basket making is appreciated as an art form, and most baskets are manufactured for their commercial value. There is a demand among collectors for this work, appreciated for its rich beauty and fine craftsmanship.

— P. Rentz

SEE ALSO:
Anasazi; Art and Design, Native Basket Maker; Pueblo.